LASKA

LASKA

*Adventures with a
Wolfdog*

BY

RONALD ROOD

W · W · NORTON & COMPANY

NEW YORK · LONDON

FIRST EDITION

THE TEXT OF THIS BOOK *is composed in photocomposition Cale-
donia. Composition, printing, and binding are by the Maple-Vail
Book Manufacturing Group. Book design by Marjorie J. Flock.*

Library of Congress Cataloging in Publication Data
Rood, Ronald N
    Laska.
    1. Wolfdogs as pets.   2. Wolfdogs—Legends
and stories.   3. Rood, Ronald N.   I. Title.
SF459.W62R66   1980   818'.5403   80–16741

ISBN 0–393–01360–X

W. W. Norton & Company, Inc. 500 Fifth Avenue, New York, N.Y. 10110
W. W. Norton & Company Ltd. 25 New Street Square, London EC4A 3NT

1 2 3 4 5 6 7 8 9 0

To Hattie and Fletcher Brown,
who have shared with us their lives,
their beloved Vermont—
and even their dog Jack—
this book is affectionately dedicated.

LASKA

And god made the beast of the earth after his kind, and cattle after their kind, and every thing that creepeth upon the earth after his kind: and God saw that *it was* good.

— Genesis 1:25

CHAPTER

I

As I write these words, one of the world's most dreaded creatures is watching me. It looks out through eyes that glint in the light of the dying fire.

Those deep-cupped ears point in my direction, alert for the faintest sound. The long, slender legs, so quiet now, could drive their owner twenty, thirty, even forty miles through the night. The jaws, among the most powerful on earth for their size, are peacefully closed. Yet quick as a shot they could snap with a force that can break the neck of a deer.

That watchful creature is the mysterious being whose long-drawn howl has struck terror in its prey through the centuries. It is that hunter whose panting breath, ever coming closer, has relentlessly followed elk and moose, bison and caribou until suddenly they could hear no more: the Spirit of the Wilderness—the great timber wolf.

The wolf is lying there and looking at me, yes, but it

9

peers out through blue eyes, rather than the golden depths that have long swept the wilderness. The graceful legs tell of power and speed, too. However, they are snowy white rather than the tan or gray or black legs that have covered so many tireless miles through the ages.

The wolf is there. And yet it isn't. Not completely, at least. It is couched in the person of a creature more closely allied to the sled dogs of the far north: that faithful companion of explorer and Eskimo for centuries, the husky.

Two generations ago, as canine lineage is figured, a full-blooded timber wolf and a purebred Siberian husky were mated at a Canadian outpost. The idea was that the wolf, bred into the sled dog line, would instill courage and power and the drive to go the farthest mile. The resulting litter was just as tough as expected. One of those half-breeds became the leader of the American racing team of Mr. John Trotier.

In due time this half-breed bore pups of her own. Their father was a powerful, blue-eyed Siberian. The offspring had the typical husky coloring of black and silver and gray.

The shape of these youngsters, however, soon told of their wild ancestry. Rangy and long-legged, the pups bore a straight tail rather than the curled husky appendage. Even as they grew, the difference between these quarter-wolves and their Siberian teammates became more pronounced daily.

✹ ✹ ✹

It was at this point that I first saw them. I paid a visit to John Trotier's kennel with an unusual request. It was a desperate one, in a way. Would he be able to help?

However, I get ahead of my story. Perhaps I'd better start at the beginning, when Stephen Greene and I visited Isle Royale National Park, in upper Lake Superior. Steve's publishing house was to publish a book I would write on some of the animals nobody loves. In his enthusiasm for the book, Steve had suggested "doing part of the wolf chapter on location."

CHAPTER

II

MIKE WOLFE slowed the outboard motor. We could see the low silhouette of the dock under the stars of the Michigan night. Mike guided our boat until it gently nudged the timbers.

"Here you are," he said. "Daisy Farm Campsite. See you shortly after sunrise."

We thanked him for the ride. "Thanks for all those wolf stories, too," Steve Greene added. "And Marie-luise's coffee."

We had spent several fascinating hours with Mike and his wife at their cottage across the bay. Mike, a post-doctoral student, was studying the timber wolf here on Isle Royale. His work was a continuation of that of Dr. L. David Mech, the author of the celebrated *Wolves of Isle Royale*.

Stephen Greene and I had been invited to walk through that wolf country. We had planned our trip for the spring; thus we'd get there before campers over-flowed the trails and sent the wolves to retreats near the center of the island. By arriving early we hoped to find signs of wolves and their enormous prey, the moose, still remaining after the snow was gone.

And so here we were, on a midnight in May, about to crawl into sleeping bags practically under the noses of those wolves.

"What do we do," asked Steve in mock concern as our only link with civilization prepared to depart, "in case of a wolf attack?"

"Nothing to it," Mike said. "Just speak in a low and reassuring tone. This'll give the wolf confidence."

With that, he pulled the starter cord. The engine sputtered to life and the boat roared off across the water.

We picked our way through the darkness to the sleeping bags. It was one of those clear northern spring nights. The frogs in a nearby swamp had been in full chorus when Mike came to take us to his cottage across the bay. Now the frogs were silent. There was scarcely a sound beyond the gentle lapping of the waves on the pebbly shore.

As I lay looking at the stars out beyond the edge of the lean-to that sheltered us, I considered the events that had brought us here. Isle Royale, its wolves and its moose were regarded as a fortuitous reply to a "what if?" question.

You know the feeling of such questions yourself: "What if I'd been born a member of the opposite sex?" "What if we lived in California instead of Connecticut?"

LASKA

"What if the speeding car that barely missed us had been a little more on target?" "What if? . . ."

Generally there can be no answer. You cannot have both sets of conditions at the same time. This has been the unfortunate case with a question asked by people interested in wildlife: "Sure, rabbits are a problem in Australia. Starlings have become a pest here. But they're foreigners in a land that has no defense against them. What if a *native* animal were freed of its enemies? Would it still become a blot on the landscape?"

There were predictions and theories, yes. Concrete proof, however, came hard. How could you keep a native animal under natural conditions—but without enemies—unless you fenced in whole mountains and lakes and forests?

That's where Isle Royale came in. Forty-five miles long and of varying widths up to nine miles, it's surrounded by the waters of Lake Superior. There's a fifteen mile swim—or a trek across winter ice—northward to the Canadian mainland. Michigan, of which the island is a part, is sixty miles across open water to the south. So a large natural biological laboratory is there for the studying, hemmed in by a nearly impassable natural "moat."

As if made to order for that classic question, a few moose somehow found their way to the island around 1910. Moose are strong swimmers; perhaps a mother and her baby crossed the open water. Or maybe a couple

14

of these huge members of the deer family walked over on the winter ice.

Those four-footed pioneers found everything to their liking. There was plenty of browse in the form of twigs of trees and shrubs. Swamps and lakeshore and inland ponds offered delicious water plants for the long-legged creatures.

And there were no enemies. No bears or mountain lions. No wolves, either.

Freed of such problems, the moose flourished. Those few became many. Every moose calf had a good chance of survival. When a yearling left its mother to seek its own fortune, it faced no hazards other than exposure to winter gales, perhaps, or the chance of a broken leg.

Yes, things were good. Too good. By the early 1920s there were an estimated thousand animals on the island, all eating and mating and having young. In less than a decade their numbers doubled. Now, held by the watery boundaries of the island, they had to scrounge for a living. There was nothing else to do. And nowhere else to go.

By the 1930s an estimated—and incredible—twenty moose inhabited every square mile of island. Competition for each mouthful of food was fierce, with the very young and the very old losing out. Resident fishermen and occasional visitors told of the stench of rotting carcasses on the beaches.

If a gust of wind took a tree down or broke off a

branch, there'd be three and four moose feeding hungrily on the twigs and leaves almost as soon as they hit the ground. The lower branches of that tree had long since been chewed back to stubs the size of a finger.

The moose had come face to face with a peril worse than any of the great carnivores: its own headlong race to starvation.

The island was at that hopeless point when I first heard of it. I was taking a college wildlife course at the time. Several tragic winters had devastated the hungry horde. The moose had crashed from perhaps four thousand animals to only five hundred just prior to 1940. "But," Professor Hosley told us, "that five hundred will build up once more. And it'll all happen again."

Undoubtedly he'd have been right if something new hadn't taken place. This was the appearance of the timber wolf. Wildlife specialists had seen what had happened when the moose had no enemies but itself; now they wondered if the presence of wolves might help bring things into balance.

Perhaps somebody quietly backed that hope with action and sneaked two or three wolves onto the island. Or possibly the wolves swam or crossed the ice, just as the moose had done years before. At any rate, a few of the creatures appeared on the island in the late forties. The large natural outdoor laboratory was about to entertain another experiment.

The wolves started in as would almost any predator:

taking the easiest prey. These were the weak, the sickly, those worst hit by grinding hunger. This, of course, left the healthier ones to survive.

Now came the next question. Faced with a burgeoning food supply, would those wolves produce a bumper crop of pups? Would these pups become parents in turn, and eat themselves out of house and home just as the moose had done?

The answer was slow in coming. Or, at least, it was slow to be discovered. There were wolf pups, but not the explosive numbers that were expected. Incredibly, although the moose were everywhere, the wolves built up their own population by slow degrees. Then they stopped.

After about twenty years, during which they could have increased to scores or even hundreds, the wolves on Isle Royale numbered only about two dozen.

Why—and how—had they regulated their numbers? This was, in part, what had brought Steve and me to the island. That and the slim chance we'd get a glimpse of one of the great creatures in the wild.

I scarcely had time to put all these thoughts together before sleep overcame me. The next morning was filled with the sounds of birds. Loons called on the lake. Ravens croaked overhead. Migratory warblers, possibly alighting with relief after the sixty miles of water from Michigan's northern peninisula, yet found energy to sing. The gray sky was rapidly turning rosy orange.

LASKA

"Twenty minutes 'til sunrise, I'd say," Steve announced, squinting at the sky. He clambered, shivering loudly, into all the clothing he had brought. "That means twenty minutes to freeze."

I grinned at him. "Think we've got time to make a pot of coffee before Mike comes to get us?"

I was struggling with the fireplace. "Lots of big wood," I said, as much to myself as to Steve. "Need some kindling to get the fire started—"

Steve's long legs had already covered half the distance between his sleeping bag and some dead brush at the edge of the clearing. All at once he stopped. "Ron! Take a look at this!"

I went over to where he was standing. Some of the meltwater from spring snows had collected in a little pool. The pool had nearly dried, leaving a layer of mud. And in the mud was the track of a great paw.

The track was about four inches in diameter. We could see the clear outline of four toes and the central pad. There were even marks where some of the stiff hairs of the animal's foot had brushed the mud.

Now it was my turn to shiver, if only from the thrill of my first wolf track. "Guess we had a visitor overnight, Steve."

For answer he pointed to another track in the moist earth. And another. "Not *a* visitor, Ron. A whole pack of them."

We tried to determine how many wolves there had been, but our tracking ability ceased at a rocky ledge.

18

There were three wolves for sure, perhaps four. "Looks as if we landed right in their living room," I said.

He chuckled. "Just so long as it wasn't their kitchen."

We followed the tracks as best we could. The wolves had apparently made a big circle well away from our slumbering forms. Here and there we could see where one had approached a bit, sniffed—then wheeled and bounded back again.

It was the closest I'd ever been to a wolf in the wild. We told Mike about it when he arrived half an hour later.

"Didn't know they were in this area," Mike Wolfe said. "But they're great wanderers. They must have known you arrived last night. Probably came snooping around to see what you were all about."

As with most wolf packs, our nighttime visitors were a family group, he pointed out, "with perhaps an extra mother-in-law for good measure."

We looked at the tracks again. Then we tucked our supplies and sleeping bags back under the lean-to and headed off across the bay.

During the winter the wolves are under daily scrutiny from the air. Not necessarily the animals themselves, but their tracks are visible in the snow. The tracks thread their way among the trees. Sometimes they are single file as when the snow is deep. Sometimes they are in a skirmish line when the animals are hunting, perhaps, or when the traveling is easy.

Nor does the discovery of a moose mean the end of

the hunt. Far from it, in fact: a moose is big as a horse. Strong as a horse, too, with piledriver hoofs that can kill a full-grown wolf with a single blow. A pugnacious bull moose or a cow defending her calf is more than a wolf pack cares to tackle.

An old or weakened moose, however, may well be fair game. The trick, of course, is for the wolves to know the difference.

"That's where 'testing' comes in," Mike told us as we pulled the boat up on shore. "The wolves find a moose track and follow it until they reach the moose. Then they test it: try to stir it to action. If it stands its ground, or even chases them, they go the other way."

"And if it runs?" Steve asked.

"—And if it runs, that's a sign of weakness. Or at least fear. So the wolves follow it to find out why it's afraid."

It was the end result of such chases that we hoped to find on our hike this morning. The plane had spotted several kills from the air. Now, with the snow gone, Mike Wolfe looked forward to viewing the remains of the moose. Close inspection might yield a clue as to why a particular animal had been singled out by the wolves.

Aided by the map that Mike carried, we were able to pick out two spots where the wolves had made a kill. Both were elderly female moose. One had a badly infected jaw. The other had a hip so riddled with disease that there was no joint left at all. Both moose must have been in constant pain. One couldn't eat; the other couldn't travel. Each was doubtless at the point of starving. The wolves had put an end to their misery. Which, we decided, was an enormous favor to those suffering animals.

In the next few days we studied several more kills. In each of them there were special conditions. One was an elderly bull moose. The old warrior must have given a good account of himself but he'd been overwhelmed at the last. Another was much younger but he'd broken a foreleg. There were also two yearlings—both separated from their mothers, perhaps, and both, therefore, vulnerable.

The average person might not have discovered the reasons behind the demise of each of these moose. To a casual eye they'd have been an impressive half-dozen wolf kills. Someone, seeing only the tragic end of the story, might have gone away with an abiding hatred for all wolves.

Mike and his associates, however, dug deeper. They analyzed the bones, the hair, the teeth of those moose. Excessive wear on the teeth here, a swelling of the joints there pointed to old age or arthritis or some other malady.

The bones are often cracked for their marrow by the powerful wolf jaws. A look at the condition of the central cavity tells of the state of the animal's health. If the cavity, ordinarily greasy from the fat of the marrow, is dry instead, it means the marrow has been absorbed. This

21

happens as a last resort by an animal in starvation. Thus a heap of bones with no great physical defect may still have a story to tell.

We saw plenty of signs of moose, too. We saw nearly a dozen of the great animals themselves. One view of that powerful body, that massive head grasping food higher than most persons could jump, was all it took to inspire great respect for the moose—and for the creature capable of bringing even one of these giants to earth.

There was little, however, to show why the wolves hadn't had their own population explosion with all this potential food walking around. The answer, we learned, was in the wolves themselves. They regulated their own numbers.

A wolf pack, it seems, is complex and intricate. The dominant male, or alpha wolf, has control over much of the pack's life. With his mate he may determine the territory for hunting. The two of them get the choicest food at a kill. It is they who produce the pups; in many instances the alpha wolf may not permit any breeding at all in the rest of the group. Hence, although a wolf pack may consist of several mature adults, the year's increase may be limited to one set of pups.

Occasionally the urge for breeding or self-assertion gets too strong. The pack may split in two. A young wolf pair may begin a family of its own away from the watchful eye of the patriarch. But the pack is ordinarily stable: in about a quarter century the wolves of Isle Royale had remained at around two dozen.

This two dozen was split into one sizeable pack with a couple of smaller ones. Each maintained its own territory, marking the boundaries in the fashion of a domestic pooch at a fireplug.

So respected are these limits that packs may seldom visit the point where two boundaries touch. Indeed, such zones of peace are often used to advantage by other animals. In Canada the deer and lesser creatures may safely live within this narrow belt. Neither pack will disturb them.

Steve and I discovered these and many other points of interest about the wolves and their prey. We were impressed with the thrift of the wolf; for instance, every available scrap would be eaten. Not only would those bones be cracked for the marrow, but sinews, hoofs, and even parts of the hide would receive a thorough chewing. When the feast was too much for one meal, the wolves might remain several days until it was completed.

We learned about the wolves, but we didn't see a single one. We found tracks everywhere, and bits of hair and those heaps of bones. "But don't worry," Larry Roop, Mike's associate, told us on our last day, "you're not alone. A physicist never sees an atom, but keeps right on studying them."

Larry, we learned, had yet to see his first wolf in the wild. Mike Wolfe had roamed the woods of Isle Royale three years before getting even a fleeting glimpse of one. But I had photographs of tracks, of bits of fur, of those impressive wilderness arenas strewn with bones and hoofs and hair. And I had a clipboard jammed with notes. So we weren't disappointed, as we bade our hosts goodbye at the dock waiting to board the seaplane.

We'd done little more than chase a will-o'-the-wisp, but it was a will-o'-the-wisp with teeth. And tracks. And "signposts" of urine, and mounds of fecal material. Plus the very real feeling that I'd see a grizzled shape, an alert set of ears, a pair of golden brown eyes peering at me around the next bend.

CHAPTER

III

THE WOLF STORY, which was the first chapter of that book about animals nobody loves, is still bringing in correspondence from readers after nearly a decade. Indeed, the whole book has proven quite durable over the years. So I'm more than gratified that Steve Greene had the idea that started it all.

Shortly after the book was published the American Bookseller's Association was due to have a convention in Boston. The Stephen Greene Press would be represented there, along with scores of other publishers. One of Steve's staff members, who was in charge of setting up the display, had a suggestion that seemed plausible enough. "Since your book will be brand new and it's about animals nobody loves," Andy Burrows said, "how about having some kind of unloved creature right there at the booth with us?"

We considered several of the stars of the book: an octopus, for instance, or an eel or a vulture. But there was a problem with each. The octopus would need a saltwater aquarium with filters and aerator. An eel was more hardy, but chances were it'd lie there like a rubber hose. And it's hard to housebreak a vulture—if you can even get one.

Which brought us around to the wolf. "That's what we need!" Andy enthused. "A real, live wolf. The ones you see on television must come from somewhere. Could you find out where, Ron?"

Maybe I could. A wolf would do wonders as a display. Besides, the teacher in me jumped at the chance to help people learn about wolves in real life. Even if not in their real surroundings.

I had several friends at zoos and wildlife organizations. So I settled down for a session at the telephone. But the odds were stacked against me. You cannot just order a wolf the way you would schedule a balloon vendor for a carnival.

My friends had wolves, all right. That wasn't the trouble. The problem was there were as many reasons against their attending our convention as there were animals.

Lobo would love to come, for instance, but he'd be out on the west coast. Sandy was to be used in a movie. Golden-eyed Amaguk was available, but three days and a few thousand visitors would be too much for her; she'd be a nervous wreck before noon of the first day. Charlie Berger's wolves were used to crowds, but Charlie was to be in Africa on behalf of a wildlife fund.

I wasn't really surprised at my lack of success. The

timber wolf is a finely tuned, exquisitely sensitive wild animal. One of the points I'd always stressed in books and talks was that a wild animal could never be expected to become a pet. A possession, yes, but not a pet. It would take a pet—and a sturdy one at that—to withstand the strain of several thousand persons peering and wanting to touch you during a convention that lasted three solid days.

I told Peg about the problems I was having. "How about a half wolf, then?" My wife suggested. "Something with enough wolf in it to make it look right but not enough to make it skittish—how would that be?"

"Fine," I agreed. But *where* would that be?"

"Oh," she said, "that's easy. Just call your friendly dogsledder."

"My what?"

"Dogsledder. You know, the fellow that has the half wolf on his dog team. Maybe he knows about something that'd fill the bill."

Peg and I had watched John Trotier and his dogs many times. Every Christmas Santa Claus arrived in a dogsled from some mysterious place behind the parking lot at a Burlington shopping center, transported by that canine conveyance. Miss Vermont rode á la Trotier's trotters, too, at a parade. John had even taken his exhibition team to Washington for Kennedy's inauguration. First in the harness these days with her powerful shoulders and tireless gait was his prized lead dog: the half-breed known as Wolf.

I gave John a call. Did he know anyone who had a half wolf we could borrow?

He promised to see if he could help me. But try as he would, he drew a blank. "I telephoned all over," he said, "but no luck. I'd almost let you take Wolf, but you'd have to take her puppies, too."

"She's got puppies?"

"Sure. Four of the cutest little creatures you ever saw. You know their father: Kimmo, my right-wheel dog. Come over and see them for yourself."

This gave us an idea. If we couldn't borrow a half wolf, how about a quarter wolf? even if it was only a puppy?

A few days later I materialized at John's home in Essex Junction. We went out to the compound behind his house. A friendly Wolf, long tail waving, nuzzled her pups as John reached down to pick one up. The pup he chose was fat and wobbly and colored like her mother: silver face and chest and paws; black ears lined with white; dark fur on the back tinged with the brown of the timber wolf.

He handed me that pup. She wiggled and squirmed and tried to bring me into focus with bleary blue eyes. How warm and solid she felt! And how wonderful!

I couldn't contain my delight. My reaction, of course, was not lost on wise old wolf-man John. "Let's see," he began, "you said you lost your dog a few months ago . . ."

"Oh, no you don't, John! All I want is to borrow a pup for a few days—not buy it!"

Pulling out a pad, John showed me the carbon copy of a sale transaction. "Ron," he said, "I'd love to lend you that puppy. I really would. But what if something happened? Or what if I sold the other three before you got her back? A single pup may be hard to sell; everybody thinks something's wrong with it."

He tapped the pad with his finger. "You see the price I got for the last pup, Ron. Cut it right in half: that's what you can have her for. Or any of the others, for that matter."

"Oh, this one's fine," I said without thinking. "She'll be just perfect."

"You sure you don't want to look at the rest of them?"

A pink tongue licked my chin. Little white feet pawed at my chest; a black nose sniffled at my face. I didn't need to answer John, and he knew it.

So I had my wolf. Even if she was only a quarter one, scarcely more than pint size and still with her mother. But what she lacked in weight, I figured, she'd make up in appeal. A puppy should win friends anywhere.

But she didn't. At least not with the authorities at the convention hall. I had filled out a questionnaire regarding facilities and equipment desired. In the blank space labeled "Other," I had indicated the need for a few square feet of floor area for "a small wolfdog puppy."

If I had said merely "puppy" it might have been all

right. But the "wolfdog" upset everything. Back came a letter on the convention center's stationery. It contained a single sentence.

"We regret to inform you," the letter stated flatly, "that the established policy of the Center does not permit wolves in the building at any time."

Then, in case I wasn't sure they meant business, it was signed "Sincerely."

Alarmed, I got my publisher on the phone. He sputtered in disbelief; then called the convention center himself.

He was back in half an hour. "Bad news, Ron. I tried to explain, but no dice. And no wolfdog."

"A ten pound *puppy?*"

"I know, Ron. I told them how nice and friendly she is, but I didn't get to first base. Perhaps it's related to the insurance."

"Insurance! For who—the people or the dog?"

There was a chance she was the only animal in the whole show, I suppose. In that case she'd need special coverage, at that. But why didn't the center's regular policy provide for such surprises? Certainly in a big building like that any number of oddball things could happen.

There are plenty of creatures that could be worse than a wolf puppy. A friend of mine has a skunk in a Bronx apartment, for instance. An uncensored skunk at that. Out they'll both go if the landlord ever gets wind of the affair. A few years ago I reached through a woven wire fence and petted a full-grown lion—in a two-car garage. And there always seem to be people who keep seals in bathtubs.

Then there was that night in Chester, Vermont. Twelve-year-old Brian wondered if I'd mind sharing the guest bedroom with Fang. I assured him it didn't matter to me, provided Fang approved. Apparently it was all right with her, too. In the morning there she lay in the sunshine: six and a half feet of boa constrictor.

Of course there was no danger. I wouldn't have hurt her for the world.

But then, I'm fond of almost any animal, wild or tame. With the people at the convention center it was different. All they had for evidence was a bit of correspondence plus a telephone call.

Besides, I felt, it went deeper than that. There was more to it than insurance, or sanitation, or whether somebody might be allergic to animal hair. Here, surfacing before we'd even brought the new arrival home from her kennel, was the age-old fear and hatred of the wolf.

Most likely the convention authorities had only seen wolves in a zoo. Perhaps the person who vetoed our plans had been denied even that slight contact. If this was true, the wolf was considered as it has been for centuries—as a shadowy, menacing creature of the night.

This was a fine turn of events. Now there was no time to look for a substitute animal. Besides, if the convention center frowned on "wolves in the building at any time" I could imagine the official reaction to an octopus. Or an eel. Or, for that matter, a flea circus—proposed, tongue in cheek, by Janet Greene when she joined her husband in suggesting creatures found in the book.

Well, I told myself, there was no loss without some gain. After all, I still had the puppy.

This brought up another problem. It was an issue I had carefully avoided. I had neglected to tell Peg I'd actually bought that puppy. She thought I was borrowing it for the convention, and would give it back when the show was finished.

We had lost our previous pet, a part beagle, several months before. Since then we'd been telling ourselves how nice it was not to have the bother of a dog. And now, thanks to me, we'd soon be right back where we'd left off.

There was another reason I hadn't told her yet. Such an important decision as a dog shouldn't be hurried. I felt somewhat sheepish about how I'd bought the little creature on an impulse. I didn't care to admit that in five minutes John Trotier had added another carbon to his sales pad. The pup was still with her mother, but John wanted me to pick her up in a couple of days. Another litter had appeared on the scene and he needed the space.

Well, might as well face it. I'd get the puppy and have her with me when I explained. Perhaps she'd help me with the sales pitch.

＊ ＊ ＊

So on that balmy spring afternoon, a small bundle of exuberance waddled toward Peg as she stepped into the kitchen after a day at school. It wagged its delight at seeing her, punctuating its joy with little wet spots all across the linoleum.

She bent down and held out her hand. "You're a cutie!" she exulted. "A real cutie!"

The puppy pounced at her hand, growling in play. Peg grimaced as sharp little teeth clamped down on her skin. "You're a wolf all right," she said. "Even if you don't look like one."

She considered the white paws, the obvious husky coloring, the transparent blue eyes so typical of the Siberian. "It's hard to believe," she said, "that this two-tone character is a wolf."

My wife tumbled the puppy over onto her back. "You're white underneath, too," she informed the little visitor. "Wherever the quarter wolf is, it's not in your color scheme."

She touseled the black ears. "You'll make a nice pup for somebody. What's your name, anyway?"

"She—doesn't have a name, Peg."

"Six weeks old and no name? John Trotier ought to have more regard for his dogs than that. When are you taking her back anyway?"

Here it came. I made a noncommital sound. And, of course, that was all my wife needed.

"You didn't—" she began. "Good Lord, you did!"

I started to explain. How John Trotier wasn't in the

33

wolf-lending business, not even in rentals. How I'd bought her before we'd known we couldn't take her with us. How I'd got her at a bargain. . . .

For answer my wife scooped up that lively bundle with one arm. She slipped the other arm around me. "Well," she said softly, "it was nice not to be bothered with a dog these past months. But I'd been secretly hoping. I guess maybe you were hoping too."

"Yep," I agreed. "I guess I was. But I didn't really get you a dog. Only three-quarters of one."

She looked down at our newest family member. "I don't know what part of you is the wolf," she said, "but break it to me gently, little Anonymous—won't you?"

IV

FIRST THINGS FIRST. No matter what was to happen, our wolfdog would need a place to sleep. And, considering her youthful status, a place to "make mistakes," as my mother charitably called those musky little offerings puppies leave in interesting places.

So we went about finding living quarters for our new star boarder. Luckily we'd not have to worry about the cold, for it was the month of May. Besides, she had been with her mother in a yard out under the pines at John Trotier's home. So she was already weatherproofed.

Good. This meant we could start with her outside. Which, we figured, was where a husky-wolf combination should be anyway.

Then we reconsidered. Too much outdoor life might slow down the housebreaking process. We wanted our animal to be completely at ease in the open, but we also wanted to keep our human friends. Friendship might be strained if we paraded a dog of nonchalant personal habits across somebody's living room rug.

LASKA

So we compromised and decided to keep her on the porch. Screened in, but projecting from the front of the house, the porch received the breeze from three sides. Hence it was practically the same as outdoors. Its wooden floor would be easy to clean; then, when our small friend became better trained, we could roll out an old carpet to make sure she'd learn to behave.

A roofed-over wooden box became her bedroom. We put in some old clothing and a small rug as bedding. We also tossed in a few cedar shavings as insurance against fleas. Although neither husky nor wolf suffer much from fleas, we hoped the aromatic mattress would keep the unwelcome guests away entirely.

To keep our wolfdog from scratching to come into the house, we put a couple of layers of chicken wire on the porch door. Thus, when she put her paws against the wire, a claw might catch for a moment. Or, at any rate, the general abrasive feeling would be unpleasant. She learned in a few days. She's never scratched at a door since. Instead she jumps up for a quick look through the door's upper glass panel. This apparition of an airborne wolfdog is a bit unsettling until you get used to it.

Now for the housebreaking part. We knew that those puppies had received some training from their mother, but that was in a yard with a dirt floor. At Trotier's, one area of the enclosure had most likely been as good for toilet use as another; our new pup had probably been taught only to keep her bed clean. Now she had to learn that most of the porch was off limits, too—and, eventually, the entire house.

We decided to follow the suggestion of a friend who raises dogs. "The first time a puppy wets on the floor," she told us, "blot up the spot with a piece of newspaper. Clean and deodorize the floor. Then place that soiled paper where you want the 'bathroom' to be. The puppy sniffs at the paper, gets the idea—and you're halfway there."

Of course the other half—getting your small charge to notify you in time to hasten her outside—might take a little effort. But at least the problem would be localized.

Don Gill, our veterinarian friend, had another comment. "The digestive system of a puppy," he said, "is straight through. There seem to be no stops and starts, no curves or bends. In one end; out the other—it's as simple as that. The minute your pup is through eating, put her outside. She'll perform almost at once. Then, Ron," he added, "you can be sure of one thing: at least *you'll* be trained."

We decided to combine our friends' suggestions. Right after our puppy was fed, she would be hoisted off the floor and hustled out the door. The result was just as Don Gill had predicted: she promptly obliged. Even if it was a command performance.

So anxious were we to be sure she didn't miss her

stride that we never failed in our part of the ceremony. And, sure enough, Don was right: *we* were trained perfectly.

The soggy newspaper routine took less of our personal energy once it was established. The first time we found one of her puddles on the floor we hastily soaked it up with last week's *Addison Independent*. Then, while Peg dried the original spot, I tenderly transported the pungent paper to the corner we'd chosen for all future deposits.

The scent trail worked well. Too well, in fact. Fifteen minutes after we'd relocated the paper it bore a gratifying new spot. But so did the original place on the floor.

We'd underestimated the sensitivity of that little black nose. The floor and the newspaper each had issued an aromatic summons—and our puppy had dutifully honored both.

We got out a bottle of pine oil disinfectant. Mixing a strong solution in water, Peg scrubbed until she was practically down to the next layer of wood. Then, as a final gesture, she sprinkled a few drops of the oil, unadulterated and unabridged, directly on the floor.

There. That should fix that square foot of space. Not even a germ would dare go near it. Neither should our wolfdog.

It was a success. Indeed, with a few short lapses of memory, the newspaper worked, too. Each subsequent mistake was carefully cleaned up and given the pine oil treatment. Within two weeks our wolfdog could have written her own book on the Where and When of House-training.

There was one unexpected and lingering effect. For more than a year, whenever a prolonged rainy spell dampened everything, the aroma of that porch somehow reminded me of a hospital.

Paper training for our new family member, with the whole outdoors waiting, was, of course, just an intermediate step—unlike the experience of a friend who lives in a New York apartment. Our friend found it difficult to take her pet to the tiny city park seventeen stories below. So the newspaper became the Great Outdoors, so to speak. Daily her small companion used the paper; daily the trash barrel received a carefully folded offering.

All was fine until one day our friend and Tupper started for a walk. Just as they stepped out of the apartment and into the hall the telephone rang. She went back to answer it, leaving the dog in the corridor. When she returned, the paper boy had apparently been there. As was his custom, he'd left the day's news in front of the door of each subscriber. And Tupper, seeing all those newspapers, knew a call to duty when he saw it. He'd manfully sprinkled every one.

As to feeding our pup, we found we had few problems. Years before, in Alaska, I had seen members of a sled team get one frozen salmon each as daily fare. Down went the salmon in hastily bitten chunks—bones and all.

39

LASKA

I knew wolves bolted their food, too. Hence, we decided to make meals as natural—and easy—as possible.

Dinner for our wolfdog, therefore, consisted of two items. One was whole milk, in case she hadn't been fully weaned when we got her. The other was meat or raw fish—which disappeared in gulps that alarmed us even though we knew the behavior was normal.

Such gastronomic feats indicated an impressive digestive capacity. And, indeed, it must have been considerable; although Peg and I saved a number of unusual items from being swallowed, many of them got away. Among those that disappeared before our wondering eyes were the following: two banana skins; chewed-up bits of twigs and branches; the hairy contents of a softball; half a bunch of carrots—tops and all; the thumb from Peg's Green Thumb glove; goodly samples of several corncobs; the leftover innards of any peanut butter jar she could find—after which she finished off the label.

We figured the label tasted good because of a lingering aroma of the oily contents of the jar. A few of her other feats, however, were harder to explain. And, one day, I thought her alimentary antics had done her in for sure.

Our wolfdog was friendly toward everyone, and we let her roam the yard. This afternoon, however, she seemed to have gone mad. Saliva drooled from her jaws. Running one way and another, she stopped to paw at her mouth; then she'd be off again.

Through long experience we've learned not to try to handle frantic animals with our bare hands. Peg disappeared for a moment; then she emerged with a couple of old jackets. Advancing in the general direction of the distraught creature, the two of us held the jackets like bullfighter's capes.

At last we cornered her against the house. "Now, keep her still," I said, "while I try to find what ails her."

Peg bore down on the struggling pup while I prepared to do a throat inspection. "Must have a bone stuck down there," I said as I bent to the task.

I knew that I wouldn't be able to feel the offending object if I stopped to put on gloves. Hoping for the best, and recalling our veterinarian friend's instructions, I placed a hand on either side of that quivering mouth. Then, pushing inward, I forced the corner of the pup's lips between her teeth. More pressure caused her to open her mouth. Now, if she closed again, she'd bite her own lips.

Holding one hand in place, I explored with the other. Nothing under the tongue. Nothing sticking into cheek or lip. And, as far as I could see, nothing caught in her throat.

I checked everything again. "It must be something she swallowed and it's down out of sight," I said. "Guess we've got to take her to the vet."

"But why's she rubbing her mouth," Peg asked, "if it's way down in her throat?"

I'd been so busy checking tongue and cheek and throat that I hadn't looked at the upper jaw. Arched across the roof of her mouth, spanning the gap between right and left sides, was a piece of springy green twig. Grasping it with thumb and finger, I pulled it free.

At once the puppy relaxed. She collapsed so completely that Peg lost her grip. "What happened?" she asked.

For answer I held up the twig. After I explained, Peg contemplated our wolfdog, serene now. "Bit off more than you could chew, didn't you?" she asked.

That rescue scene, I figured, helped our wolfdog discover her place in the scheme of things. It showed her that I had the "upper hand." She learned still more when Jerry, a peppery little terrier, gave her an unexpected lesson.

Jerry belonged to our friends the Flemings. He was inquisitive, irrepressible, and invincible. The world existed solely for him. When the Flemings came to call we'd hastily check everything edible, breakable, and all but inflammable. Jerry had a way of going through a house like a horde of army ants; with him, nothing was sacred.

That June day we heard the slam of a car door. Almost immediately the screen door of the porch burst open—as luck would have it, it wasn't latched—and we heard the clicking of tiny nails. Then came a despairing puppy wail, followed by the barking of a terrier.

♉ ♉ ♉

We stepped out onto the porch. Jerry stood three feet from our wolfdog's box, tail wagging so hard his hind end went with it. From inside the box came menacing puppy growls. And looking out from the darkened interior were two blue eyes.

He wagged and she growled. He dropped down on his chest, his nether portion high in the air, tail whirling like a helicopter. He whined and barked and invited her to come out and play. But she just growled.

I tried to coax the unwilling wolfdog from her lair. She obliged only after I had evicted Jerry from the porch. Even then, as we showed her off, her main concern was for the commotion on the other side of the porch door.

After awhile Jerry had calmed down a bit, and we decided to reintroduce the two dogs. It was a repeat of the first time. She yelped and snapped and beat a retreat to the box again. Jerry couldn't have weighed more than twenty pounds to her fifteen, but she would have none of him.

On a subsequent meeting with Jerry she tried to hide behind me. In her case, a little humility was doubly important. In her mind, it seemed, I had magically extracted the painful twig and I'd "driven" Jerry off the porch when he first threatened her. Such events, apparently, helped establish me as the alpha wolf of our little "pack." And Peg was obviously my mate.

Despite our pup's vocal objection when threatened

43

by Jerry she was, for the most part, surprisingly quiet. Almost alarmingly so. Most puppies yelp and howl and cry when they're consigned even to such a commodious space as a porch. Ours would merely gaze after our retreating forms as we'd close the door. Then, with a sigh, she'd settle down at the entrance to her box. Such behavior might be expected in a grown animal, but we found it disconcerting in a youngster not yet three months of age.

Then we considered just what this behavior might mean. I had told her to hush once or twice when we first established her on the porch. The dog in her would scarcely have heard such an admonition, but the wolf listened more alertly. My "be quiet!" was a firm command—like the warning growl of the she-wolf, perhaps. Instinct told her it was meant to be heeded.

V

WHEN OUR WOLFDOG outgrew her porch, how would she fit in around our Vermont home? She already roamed the lawn much of the time and I knew she'd probably take readily to our fields and forests. Together with the New Haven River that ran along our eastern boundary, these hundred acres should delight any pup. But it was what went with our land—and our way of life—that caused me to stop and think.

All those rocky ledges and riverbanks and hollow trees and grassy meadows held a multitude of living creatures. We wondered how our new family member would get along with her wild neighbors. Rebel, our former semibeagle, had done fine. However, that was at least partly because he'd broken a hip when small and it had never healed right. Much of the time he walked around on three legs. Thus he could be outdistanced easily by woodchucks or squirrels.

Rebel even stood on his front feet and twisted his

body to supply that time-honored doggy "signature" on a fence post or auto tire. Such a performance was an efficient way of dealing with his handicap even if it was a bit startling to behold.

Barring some disability, would our canine companion match Rebel's forced good behavior when it came to a running rabbit, say, or a bounding deer?

There was no way to tell, of course. But if our small pup grew to be anything like her mother, she'd weigh seventy or eighty pounds, all of it ready for the trail. Or to make a new trail, for that matter.

Even if we could train the wolf in her—as well as the dog in her—to let the creatures of the Vermont countryside go their way unharmed, another question presented itself: how would she react to people?

Seldom a day goes by that Peg and I don't have several visitors; sometimes there are many. How might a creature combining the wildness of the wolf with the work seriousness of the sled dog get along with strangers on a daily basis? There were also the youngsters who might impulsively throw their arms around her. Would she merely grunt like a placid old shepherd dog? Or would she resent the familiarity?

A wolf has a wilderness way of looking at things. Its life may depend on instant action. The animal may need the curiosity to investigate an unknown situation one time but to flee in haste the next. A dog, with its reflexes dulled by centuries of domestication, might not be nearly as sensitive.

Would some unexpected turn of events terrorize our wolfdog? Would loud noises, perhaps, or sudden motions send her cringing into a corner? Or might they make her completely unmanageable?

No point in guessing the answers to all these questions. We'd have to wait to see how she turned out. But we couldn't refer to our wolfpup as "her" and "she" any longer. What she needed was a name.

Small as she was, and falling all over herself when she tried to run, she was a candidate for puppy names like Bungle or Muddles—or even Puddles. But we had to bestow on her a name that would someday fit what we hoped she'd be: a dignified lady. And a quarter wolf to boot.

Friends who are dog fanciers suggested: "Look back in her pedigree. Dog breeders often name a puppy after another dog a few generations back. You can find good names, sometimes."

My neighbor agreed. "I deal with them all the time in breeding cattle for our farm. You get a little family tree like 'Out of Meadowgold by Sunshine' or 'Out of Invincible, by Supplanter.' What you seldom get is 'Out of Debt by December.' "

I explained that, whatever else our newest pet might possess, a pedigree was not one of them. As John Trotier had told me in explaining her ancestry, "The American Kennel Club does not recognize wolves."

However, John had given me several sets of documents relating to other members of his sled teams, so we spread the papers out on the table. They bore impressive titles, indeed: Czar Ivanivitch, for instance, and Hermanasita of Monadnock. Now and again there was something simple, like Jack or Domino, but it'd soon be balanced off by Akiak of Anadyr and Champion Ivanka of Kabkol.

It sounded like a fruitful family tree. Unpronounceable, too. We didn't want to have to go to the back door and call "Here, Dushakovich!"

Then we found the perfect name. It fitted the wolf in our animal and the husky in her as well. Back in 1953, the Monadnock Kennels had served as matchmaker between two Siberians. The father, or sire, was known as Petya. The mother, or dam—and there it was—bore the name of Laska.

The word "Laska" seemed to fulfill our expectations: freely translated from the original Eskimo name for our forty-ninth state, it meant "the Great." And so "Laska" she became.

We still had to find out how Laska would fit into our land and our lives. Her playfulness, for instance, was oddly tempered with timidity. One day she attacked an old rag in the garage. Growling hideous puppy threats and terrorizing the rag, she shook it and tossed it as she started out into the yard.

The rag caught on a projection of the garage door track. Snarling at the recalcitrant piece of cloth, she pulled. It tore asunder with a great ripping sound—and she fled in dismay.

She'd never had a rag—or a door, for that matter— that talked back at her before. Nor, apparently, did she care to repeat the experience. Peg saw her later that day, just starting to enter the garage. Laska went as far along the other side from the offending door as possible— walking as fast as a three-month puppy could, while still keeping her dignity.

The gentleman who came for a visit was also more than she'd bargained for. He was left over from the winter, so to speak, although it was July. The morning was cool—indeed, we've had frost in these Vermont hills about one July in four—and he honored the occasion by wearing a raccoon coat.

Laska knew nothing of the man's attire as he drove up into our yard. She romped joyously around his van as it came to a halt. Then she stood expectantly, tail waving and tongue lolling, waiting for the door to open.

Gene Lavalley is a big man. And he was twice as big in his 'coonskin coat. As he got out of the car, our flab- bergasted pup took one look at all that fur—and scuttled away in terror. She ki-yi-yied out beyond the blueber- ries. Still running, she disappeared into the tall grass.

Her progress was marked by the violent behavior of the greenery as it went down under her onslaught. Twice she jumped up above the grass. Each time we were treated to a brief glimpse of a wide-eyed face, look- ing to see if she was being followed.

Impressed, Gene stared at her retreating form. "What the heck ails her, Ron?"

LASKA

"Dunno, Gene. Unless it's your coat."

He chuckled. "Probably thinks it's the biggest racoon she ever saw."

I called to the panicky pup. She came doubtfully to the edge of the lawn. While Gene elaborately took off the coat and draped it over a nearby bush, I spoke words of great consolation to Laska. Then we retired to a couple of lawn chairs a short distance away to see what would happen.

She looked at the coat awhile. Then, watching warily, she began a wide and cautious circle of the fuzzy apparition. Apparently there was no expected animal scent, so she gingerly approached to where she could sniff a sleeve.

There must be a sneaky sadistic streak in me somewhere. I picked up a pebble. Just as the wary wolfdog made contact with the fur, I lobbed the pebble. It hit the coat with a small thud—and the poor pup did a somersault. She scrambled to her feet, all paws going, and fled in consternation once more.

When she returned a second time we let her investigate undisturbed. Apparently satisfied the coat meant no harm, she lay down on the lawn. But one watchful eye kept track of the garment, and two black ears with their white fur lining remained cocked in its direction.

At last Gene got up to leave. "Here, girl," he said, pointedly showing Laska the coat as he hung it over his arm. "Nothing to fear—see?"

✹ ✹ ✹

We figured she had struck a truce with the overcoat as she scarcely gave Gene or his garb a glance—until he started the car. Then she pursued it down the driveway. Snarling and snapping and barking, she told the retreating raiment what'd happen if it ever invaded her haunts again. Having vanquished her gigantic enemy, she returned in triumph.

It was the only car she ever chased out of the yard.

That youthful exuberance kept popping up, however. She tried her teeth on almost anything—the usual shoes and slippers, for instance, plus the handle to Peg's pocketbook. She also thoughtfully punctured the garden hose along half its length so the lawn looked like Yellowstone when we turned on the water.

Then there was the hammer. With Laska as an interested spectator, I'd been using the hammer for a repair job. Peg called me away from work for a few minutes. When I got back, the hammer was missing.

In the time I'd been gone, the wolf had made a kill. She'd severed the hammer's jugular vein and dragged the carcass off into a corner. There she'd gone to work on that tough hickory handle. Those sharp white teeth had chipped away at the wood until splinters dotted the floor. Now she was intent on finishing it off.

As I contemplated the demise of the hammer handle, I thought again of the wolves on Isle Royale, cracking those massive moose bones. This, in turn, reminded me of something that happened at John Trotier's house.

51

LASKA

I had gone to visit him one day when he was about to give a chunk of bone and gristle to Wolf and her brood. It looked like a standing rack of mutton, minus the flesh. When he brought the puppies out for me, one of them seized it. With playful baby growls, the youngster clamped onto its prize. Explaining to the puppy that the huge chunk was for its mother, John grabbed one end and pulled. The puppy pulled in return—and was lifted right off its feet.

"Heck, Ron," said my host, noting my surprise, "A bulldog's got nothing on these little fellers. Watch this."

With that he shifted hands. Now he was holding the pup by the scruff of the neck. Then he released the meat—but the quarter wolf hung on just the same. That massive chunk must have weighed as much as the puppy. And there they were: John holding the pup who held the meat.

He set his double burden on the ground. Then he walked over to the puppy's mother, who'd been watching the proceedings. "Wolf," he said, pulling back her lips to look at the long white teeth, "I'm sure glad you're on my side!"

Now, a few weeks later, I saw that power for myself in another of Wolf's offspring. I decided I had better draw the line right now. "Laska!" I said sharply, as I reached for the hammer. "*No!*"

The effect was like a shock. Laska recoiled as if she had been struck. She crouched low, watching. Not a muscle of her stirred as I picked up the hammer. Those bleak blue eyes looked at me, unblinking.

Then, perhaps in response to some unconscious signal I sent out, she rose to her feet. Tail at uncertain half mast, pink tongue appearing apologetically first on one side of her mouth and then the other, she started forward. Curious as to what would happen, I made no sign. So she sank down again.

I'd punished her enough. "Okay, girl," I said—and had hardly gotten the "O" out before she'd crashed into me, waggling her exuberance at having been forgiven.

That was all it took. She had learned, just like that. The episode taught her the meaning of the word "no." Since then I've had occasion to use the term many times. It's so effective, indeed, that we use it only sparingly. Otherwise the impact of the command might be lost.

Laska had learned something, and so had I. I realized one more reason the wolfdog cross could be expected to do well on a sled team. The wolf, being a member of a pack by nature, almost automatically takes its place—as soon as it determines exactly what that place may be. The other portion of its bloodline, the husky, has taken orders for untold centuries. The combination should make an animal of surpassing loyalty and obedience.

Notice, however, that little word "should." These are living creatures. They haven't read the book on how they should act. Not everything, always, falls in place.

Over the weeks we tried to determine what was wild

and what was domestic in our new pup. Any canine youngster could be expected to nibble on a hammer handle, for instance. It was the way Laska nearly demolished it that was so surprising. This, we knew, showed the power built into those wide jaws with their peculiar musculature.

She had also howled soon after we got her. It was just a short howl; scarcely the long drawn wail I had heard in Alaska years before. It was higher-pitched, too, but it had a wildness that somehow went right through us. Although the month was May, we could see—and hear—some imaginary hunt in a forgotten forest.

Other than these events, however—plus her argument with the raccoon coat—we'd not discovered much that would suggest "wolf" instead of "dog." Nor was there anything to suggest any kind of conflict between a domestic ancestry of more than a thousand years and a wild heritage that stretched infinitely farther than that. The wolf and the dog seemed perfectly blended in a single animal.

Which goes to show how little we knew.

They say a puppy will grow to fit its feet. Big puppy feet, big dog. If so, Laska had plenty of potential. Those four white paws were forever getting in her way. It seemed as if she was wearing snowshoes. Or, at least, ski boots. Sometimes she'd stumble over herself in full gallop, as it were. Then she'd take a header, or maybe half sit with her tangled hindquarters while her front feet valiantly continued their race. Obviously, however, when she got those feet straightened out, she'd have a good deal of speed. The legs of both the wolf and the husky are long and slender and capable of mile after mile without slackening.

We hadn't thought much about Laska's running potential. After all, we'd got her for a book exhibit, not for a sled dog. Nor did we intend to let her roam our woodlands. We'd done everything we could to encourage the wildlife on our hundred acres.

We had set out food plants and cleared openings in the deep woods for shubbery to grow. We had left ancient hollow trees standing to provide animal dens. Hi Monroe had put in a small pond for us; its quiet waters played host to duck and mink and muskrat. A nature trail threaded its way through our private wildlife sanctuary. The last thing we needed was some strange kind of hybrid romping around and upsetting the forest.

At the moment, however, all we had was about fifteen pounds of lovable puppy. But she was growing fast. This was brought home to me one day in July.

On that morning I was writing at the picnic table on the front lawn. The birds were singing in the maples and in the shrubbery at the edge of the river. A hawk circled overhead. Somewhere a cowbell tinkled. A rooster crowed on a farm up the valley. Now and again I struck a word on the typewriter, but progress was slow. There were too many delights to see and hear.

LASKA

It was a perfect setting to be writing an article about the Vermont countryside. Too perfect. This I knew the moment Peg came to the front door. She spoke only one word: "Ronald!"

A moment like that tells me why nicknames are popular. It's because given names aren't. You get called by your formal given name when you've done something wrong. Not by your nickname. Or at least that's how it's been with me. Turning around, I looked at Peg inquiringly.

"Your wolf has done it this time!" she stated.

"*My* wolf? She's your wolf, too!"

"Oh, no. Not now she isn't!" And with that enlightening news she disappeared.

Placing a book on the papers by the typewriter so my story wouldn't fly away, I dutifully went into the kitchen to see what *my* wolf had done. When I got there nothing seemed amiss. No curtains pulled off the windows. No newspaper in shreds. No shoe with a newly ventilated toe. Not even a suspicious spot on the floor.

"Well?" I asked Peg. "What'd she do, anyway?"

For answer, my wife glared at our small wolfdog. Laska lay in the corner by the back door, head pressed down onto her paws. She looked meekly from Peg to me and back again.

"Remember that partridge and her babies up at the edge of the woods?"

Of course I remembered them. We'd been overjoyed

when we'd stumbled upon the female ruffed grouse with her handful of chicks last week. Although there were perhaps a dozen babies, they had flown and scampered away in such a flurry that we'd lost track of every one.

When the leaves had settled back to earth and the bushes quit shaking, all that seemed to be left of the little family had been a brown bird the size of a small chicken. She cried piteously and dragged a "broken" wing as she tried to lure us away from the scene. There was no sign of her chicks, although we knew that little brown eyes were peering at us from beneath leaves, behind rocks, and even in the crotch of some nearby tree.

"Sure, Peg." I answered. "I remember the grouse. What about it?"

My wife removed a hand from behind her back. In it was what looked like a speckled pigeon. But I knew, with sinking heart, that it was no pigeon. It was the mother grouse.

I gently took the bird. Its warm brown coat was dotted with black and buffy white. The ruff on either side of its neck, composed of twenty or so dark feathers right and left, lay lifeless just above the shoulders. The head dangled limply, its jaunty crest now lying flat. The bright eyes that missed almost nothing in life were glazed and unseeing in death.

Peg reached forward and spread the bird's tail. It fanned out in a wide arc of about twenty square-tipped feathers, crossed by half a dozen narrow dark bands. The band near the tip was much wider and bore the proof I hoped would not be there: a single feather that lacked color so the band appeared broken. We'd noticed it on the female the other day—and here it was in our hands.

Perhaps the bird had flown into a tree trunk. Possibly Laska had found it dead on the ground. But a sickening crunch when I pressed the bird's sides told me what must have happened. That grouse had given her life for her family. And undoubtedly it was Laska who had taken it from her.

I looked over at our wolfdog. Only a four-month puppy, and she'd outwitted one of the most sagacious creatures in the woods.

We would probably never know how she'd done it. Perhaps she had crept up behind a log or bush and pounced without warning. Possibly the mother, in play-ing wounded, had strayed too close. Or maybe, as happened once with a farm boy I heard of, one of the youngsters had been captured, whereupon the female flew to the attack.

With the farm boy that grouse had gained her end: the startled lad dropped the chick and ran. If this female had tried it, however, she had gambled and lost.

Today it was but a bird in the bush, plus the orphan-ing of a dozen babies. Tomorrow it might be bigger game. There had to be some way to stop it.

From the looks of our pup, Peg had already chastised

❧ ❧ ❧

her. I was about to add my own brand of malediction when a thought struck me. At least she'd brought her victim back to the house. If I laced her out too well, perhaps when she pulled her next stunt she'd keep it a secret.

Yet she had to be taught. As I considered how this would be accomplished, the experience of a friend came to mind. He'd once had a bird dog that kept getting side-tracked by rabbits. Perhaps the solution he had discovered would work now.

One of the grouse's wings had been almost severed at the last joint. I completed the job. Hastily snatching a piece of string from the kitchen drawer, I advanced on Laska. "No!" I said, waving the wingtip before her nose. "*No!* No grouse—never again!"

She got up to run, but I grabbed her collar. Then I scratched her nose with that sheaf of feathers. "*Understand?*"

While still reading the riot act, I tied the wingtip to Laska's collar. There it would stay for several days, a reminder to her sensitive nose that grouse were highly undesirable elements in this world. And to make sure she did not forget, I'd remove it a couple of times daily, remind her about it, and attach it again. This I'd do until she was supposedly sick of "grouse" and all that it meant.

I wasn't sure it would work. However, my sportsman friend said a rabbit's foot used in the same way would keep his bird dogs honest. It'd be worth a try, I figured. Besides, there should be little harm in it. The dog apparently gets disgusted at the offending fur or feathers, rather than at the person who ties them on.

Laska carried her embarrassing burden for nearly a week. After what seemed a suitable time, I removed the grouse wing. I hoped she'd learned her lesson.

She may have learned, but I wasn't so sure about myself. After all, it's in a dog's nature to chase anything that moves. And that would go double for a wolf. So it was up to me to keep those natural urges within bounds.

Indeed, as I considered further, a disquieting thought came over me: the loss of that grouse was my fault as much as hers. And if we didn't control her, what would be next?

CHAPTER

VI

GOOD HEAVENS, DAD! What happened to your dog?"

Our daughter Janice had just driven across the bridge and up the driveway. She got out of the car and looked apprehensively behind her.

"What do you mean, 'what happened?' She's fine, as far as I know."

Our daughter started to reply. Then she hastily bent down, hands spread before her. She looked ready to ward off an attack.

Laska came bounding joyfully around from behind the car. "Maybe *she's* fine, Dad," Janice said, "But I'd like to see the other guy."

One look and I understood. Laska's white paws and black coat had taken on a new color: brown. The brown was smeared in gobs on her fur. Matted into it were pieces of grass and weeds.

River mud. Unless I was mistaken, our pup had been in a tussle under the bridge. And Janice's thoughts about

LASKA

the other fellow had doubtless come from the appearance of our wolfdog's face. There was a gash on her lip, and another on her nose. Her white cheeks and muzzle were flecked with blood.

Perhaps she'd been in the middle of a scrap when Janice's car had come across the bridge. The rumbling of the wheels on the planks may have stopped it all. But what was she fighting? And why?

Telling my daughter to hang on to Laska for a minute, I ran into the house for the leash. Then, snapping it in place, I took our contentious canine down the path that led under the bridge. Close behind us came Peg and Janice. They were probably fearful of what they'd find, just as I was—and even more fearful that they'd find nothing. The latter case might mean Laska's antagonist had gotten away to suffer. Or perhaps to die.

It didn't take long to piece together what had happened. Laska led us right to the spot. There were obvious signs of a scuffle along the edge of the bank. We could make out the prints of Laska's paws in the mud. There were other paw prints, too—smaller, strong-clawed, with evidence of furry webbing between the toes.

Laska had surprised a muskrat. Perhaps it had been chewing greenery on the bank. Or perhaps it had been in the shallow water along the shore when she saw it and pounced on it. Although the New Haven River was faster running than the usual swamp or pond favored by these rodents, one or two would work its way along the

✿ ✿ ✿

shore each year. Probably they're youngsters out to seek their fortunes; muskrat family ties become a bit strained when the first litter is a month old and the second one is on the way.

Laska might have surprised this muskrat. But I'll bet the surprise wasn't all one-sided. Three pounds of irate muskrat can be a terrible opponent. In fact, from the hesitation in our dog's manner as she sniffed around the scene, I suspect she was lucky the car rattled across the bridge when it did. It gave her an excuse to leave.

Once my son and I were walking along a road by a pond. On the other side of the road was an area that bore a few cattails. In spring it probably held water, but on that summer day it was dry. As Tom and I walked past the spot, we saw a muskrat poking along through the cattails. It spotted us the same moment—and charged.

Doubtless we seemed to be a threat because we were between the muskrat and the water. "Watch it!" I yelled.

I managed to sidestep those chattering jaws. My eight-year-old son wasn't so lucky. Failing to size up the situation, he just stood his ground. The muskrat flung itself on his leg, and buried its teeth in his boot.

Still uncomprehending, Tom stared down at his furry opponent. Luckily, the creature had attacked the upper front of the boot. Laces, eyelets, and boot tongue all interfered with a good chomp. By the time I'd recovered my own senses enough to aim a kick in the direction of the muskrat, it had released its hold and escaped.

LASKA

I knew the muskrat had missed when I heard Tom's delighted remark at the close of it all. "Gee, Dad," he exulted, "he was *friendly!*"

So, if this muskrat had been just as "friendly," Laska had gotten more than she'd bargained for. It wasn't all bluff and no bite, as with that ruffed grouse. Perhaps our bloodied and apprehensive predator had even come out second best.

Nevertheless, we couldn't put up with Laska's hunting behavior. Although we hadn't known about the existence of the muskrat, there were other animals our wolf-dog would meet sooner or later. There was a den of foxes on the north hillside, for instance. Plus a mother raccoon and her three youngsters in the old hollow spruce. The woodchuck at the edge of the meadow. Snowshoe hares. Skunks. Deer mice. And even deer.

The next step was clear. If our wolf pup was on a collision course with the countryside, she'd have to be controlled. But, with Peg and me traveling over much of America on tours and visits to camps and schools, control wouldn't be easy. What would we do when we were off to Virginia, say—hire a sitter?

No. Control meant more than just keeping an eye on our irrepressible pup. Merely knowing where she was would not be enough. Certainly not right now, at any rate, while she and the juvenile wildlife populations were both getting their wings, so to speak.

It reminded me of one time Peg and I were visiting

Dick and Freda King. Three of their four children had fairly well flown the family coop, but small Susie was still toddling around and getting into mischief. "Dick," Freda called from the kitchen, "watch your daughter."

Dick and I were buried deep in the Sunday paper. My host raised his eyes long enough to look in the direction of the kitchen. "Watch her do what?" he inquired.

That, I knew, would be the case with the average dog sitter. Already Laska had demonstrated a disconcerting ability to go her own way. What if the sitter let her take a little run—and a bounding rabbit crossed her path? I could see the resulting high-speed chase: rabbit leaping in front, sitter yelling in back, with dog cavorting in the middle—eyes straight ahead and deafer'n a post.

Or perhaps even invisible. We had seen the phenomenon several times already and were to be presented with it many times in the future: Laska's disappearance in what was apparently plain sight. She'd be trotting toward a bush or tree in a field, say—and then she would be gone.

A few moments later she'd reappear, still headed in the same direction but several hundred feet farther away. In the interval she'd have pursued a course that kept the tree between her and us. Thus her progress was masked by the intervening greenery.

Usually there was no apparent need for such guile. Laska might turn shortly and come loping back. But she did it all so easily and naturally that we figured this was one of the wild traits handed down to her by her half-wolf mother.

I've seen foxes and coyotes take advantage of natural cover in the same way. For that matter, the ruffed grouse is an expert at it too. Many a hunter has plugged a tree trunk as one of these canny birds rocketed away in a roar of wings. Its flight path left no room for a clear shot until the grouse veered out of sight.

So, with a pet that could go conveniently deaf when you called, plus the ability to "make believe she isn't there," as one youngster described Laska's disappearing act, we couldn't let her run. Not even if we taught her perfect obedience. We couldn't keep her chained, either. Nor could we keep her in the house.

This was a fine situation. Here we were, out in the open country, with acres of woods and fields and meadows just waiting for a frolicking dog. And yet she couldn't frolic. "Not," said Peg, "if we want to be fair to the rabbits and woodchucks and baby birds."

"But, Mom," Janice said, "Laska cannot help the way she is."

"I know she can't help it," Peg agreed. "But *we* can."

Of course our pet was merely behaving like most other dogs. Only more so. Her wildness was just closer to the surface, that's all. A city-bred Chihuahua may find no more challenging prey than a fly at the window but it can go after that fly like a fox after a quail. And any game

warden can recite stories of gentle, well-fed house pets
in full cry after a fleeing deer.

"One of the saddest things I ever had to do," a warden friend told me, "was to shoot a champion retriever.
It had won a whole roomful of ribbons and trophies. That
dog represented hundreds of dollars of love and effort
and training. Yet there it was—right on top of a downed
half-grown fawn."

Indeed, as we considered further, the whole idea of
the country as the proper place for pet dogs—and cats—
warranted a second look. The mouse or chipmunk captured by a joyful dog or a watchful cat is making the
supreme sacrifice as surely as that fawn. Fido or Tabby
may pounce in play; the hapless victim dies in earnest.

Nor would it be sufficient to shrug it off "because
that's the way our pet is made." Not for us, at least.
Maybe our pet couldn't help it, true. But, as Peg had
said, *we* could.

A friend of ours had a pasture full of red cedar trees.
He cut and trimmed and sold them for posts. We bought
a dozen ten-footers and a big roll of heavy fencing. Then
I set out to make a yard for Laska.

The yard was laid out among the red pine trees behind the house. Our son who worked for a carpenter,
volunteered to make a doghouse suited to its special occupant. "I've got just the materials," Roger said.
"They're left over from a job we did in Middlebury."

LASKA

Sure enough, the finished house was a credit to its builder. And to its new occupant. Constructed of two-by-four and scraps of plywood, it was roughly a four-foot cube. It had a broad, sloping roof so our dog could slumber on it, Snoopy style.

It was the north side, however, that really gave the house character. Roger had that side in mind when he offered to build the thing. There it stood, a leftover piece of plywood that had served as a sign for an enterprising couple who'd scrounged up enough money to build a new home. In bold red letters it declared for all to see: "FLEA MARKET."

And how did Laska like her new quarters? "Take a look," said Peg.

We had enticed her into the yard with a tasty bone. Then we'd left her to get used to the place. Now, an hour later, I peeked out a window. Laska was racing around the enclosure as if bereft of her senses. She dashed out under the pines, veered away just before the fence, and careened off in the direction of the hardhack bush. A leap on top of her new mansion—and back she'd go for another round.

Her antics were only half of it. The other half consisted of what she carried. In her headlong rush she picked it up, dropped it, picked it up again: one of last year's pine cones.

The cone of a red pine is nearly as broad as it is long when its scales are open. Hence it is almost round in shape. Those opened scales even give it a spring when it hits the ground, so it is a natural bouncing ball. And there was our underprivileged pup—tossing the "ball," enjoying herself immensely, and scarcely aware she wasn't free. All it took was a dried pine cone.

She played with the cone several times that day. Apparently discovering it anew each time, she'd throw it in the air, catch it at full speed, drop it, miss it intentionally on the pickup, double back, whirl,—her game was endless.

Days later, after the cone was soggy and minus half its scales, she still searched it out. However, it was less cooperative about bounding, so I decided to get her a ball of her own.

That was my mistake. Not in getting the ball, but in the ball I got. It was a solid rubber ball, the best one in the pet store. Unpainted, it was certified "nontoxic and recommended for dogs at play," according to the tag on the mesh bag in which it was sold. The problem was it hadn't been correctly labeled. The tag should have said "educational toy." Educational for me, a least. I let Laska out of her yard, threw the ball down the driveway—and learned my lesson.

Away went dog and ball. Just as with the pine cone she tossed it and caught it and dropped it and circled around it and ran away and came back again. Farther she ran, off through the meadow grass. I watched in dismay, like a kid after an escaping balloon.

LASKA

Then, all at once, she was trotting back toward me. Empty-mouthed.

I had no idea where that ball had been dropped. I tried to enlist her aid in looking, but she was no help. Her puppy attention span had stretched to its limit and snapped. So I poked around in the greenery while she helpfully plunged after crickets. Have you ever tried to find a neutral-colored ball, tastefully camouflaged with a coating of grass and saliva, down among the grassroots?

So much for that educational toy. Since then I've bought several balls for Laska. They've been the kind that can be seen in high grass or down under a bush: shocking pink or hot orange, or sizzling red. And, most likely, bad for her innards.

But it probably doesn't matter how nutritious they are. They're usually lost in a week, anyway.

As the days passed, we realized the yard was working out better than we'd dared to hope. She was very much at home. Perhaps it was the forested feeling of being under the pine trees. Perhaps it was the roof where she sat like a sentinel for hours. Or perhaps it was the unobtrusive presence of that fence, far enough not to crowd her but near enough to give a sense of security.

Her feeling of being at home may have been helped by her favorite old rug. We had taken the rug that had been in her box on the porch and tossed it on the floor of her house. We've often used a trick like this with other animals when they've been placed in strange surroundings. Bring along something that's saturated with their smell and putting it in before we introduce the animal, we figure, makes it a sort of welcome mat.

Over the weeks, the rug came apart. Then the two halves began to disintegrate. "Why not give her some hay?" Peg asked. "Then she can fix it up to suit herself."

Willie Sumner had been cutting the hay on our meadows to feed his beef cattle. We swapped the hay for some beef each year—and everybody was happy. So we had Willie leave half a dozen bales on his last pass through the field. I took one of them, broke it open, and poked the whole thing into Laska's house.

She sniffed suspiciously at first. Then into the house she went. All was quiet for perhaps thirty seconds. We heard a dull thump: one of the chunks hitting the wall. Then there was the sound of hay in great agitation. Then another thump, and another.

A chunk came rolling out the door. It was followed by a cloud of dust. Out through the cloud poked Laska's head. She sneezed violently, looked at us wildly, grabbed the hay, and disappeared.

More sneezes. More thumps. Now and again we'd catch a glimpse of a white paw or a waving tail. Once or twice she looked out through the gloom. Then she'd disappear to renew the battle.

It took her a week to arrange the furniture. I looked inside the first afternoon; she'd put her bed in the back left corner. Something must have been wrong with the arrangement, however, for there was more sneezing and rustling the next day. Later inspection showed the bed had migrated to the right rear. Two dozen sneezes later it moved forward, just inside the door.

Perhaps this was too drafty. Maybe it lacked privacy. Snuffling and raising more dust, she finally settled on the only remaining corner: the left front. There she shaped a little nest as big as a dishpan to fit her curled-up body. Apparently this was just the right location. As she grew, the nest grew, but it stayed in the same spot, summer and winter.

Good. We'd made a comfortable home for our pet. We had taken care of the homemaker in her. Apparently the dog in her was satisfied, too.

So was the wolf in her. For the moment, at least. But there was one thing not yet settled. Peg had mentioned it without realizing on that day she had inquired of Laska which part of her was the wolf.

Laska, of course, had given us no reply. She was but a tiny thing then, but now she was growing up.

And she was about to give her answer.

CHAPTER

VII

I AWOKE WITH A START. My heart was pounding and there was a prickly feeling along my spine.

Something was in the room. Or perhaps it was just outside. There had been a noise, I knew. But what kind of noise I could not say.

I lay there a few moments, trying to put my thoughts together. Then, slowly, I turned my head. There was no unusual sound, save the throbbing of my own pulse.

Through the gloom I could just make out a dark object in the corner. That would be the bookcase. Further along the wall was Peg's closet, then mine. Then the tall rectangle that was the door.

Nothing unusual there. I carefully surveyed the rest of the room: two bureaus, the little table, silhouettes of plants on the windowsill. Nothing extra; nothing out of place.

Unconvinced, I reached for the flashlight. Feeling foolish and yet needing to put my mind at ease, I prowled about the house. Kitchen, fireplace, bath, big room that opened out on the deck—all were peaceful and in order. The guest wing, my office, our little greenhouse—all quiet and undisturbed.

Perhaps I'd been dreaming. The thump or the scream or the crash or whatever it was might have been the climax to some nightmare. After all, such illusions can seem so real they wake you with a nameless dread.

Yes, I decided, that's what it must have been. When I was a child, I'd occasionally had bad dreams. Too much Fourth of July did it to me once. Another time the weather had changed and snowflakes had drifted in through the open window. They'd settled on my face and I had wakened with the feeling of being attacked.

Well, so much for the whatever-it-was that had startled me. I put the flashlight on the nighttable and carefully slipped back into bed. Peg mumbled something, shifted position, and continued her snooze.

I was just about to return to my own slumber when an owl hooted. And right away the mystery was solved.

It wasn't the owl hoot that gave me the answer, however: it was what followed. Starting low, almost imperceptibly, then rising as it gained in pitch and volume, and dying away into the silence, a lonely wail drifted on the night air—the howl of a timber wolf.

It lasted perhaps ten seconds. I tried to shake my wife awake. "Peg! Hear that?"

"Hear what?" she asked with her head buried in the pillow.

"Wolf call," I said. "Quick—listen to Laska!"

By the time Peg was alert, that cry of the wilderness had faded off into the night. The silence closed in once more.

"Okay," she said. "I've listened to her. Now can I go back to sleep?"

"No, Peg. It's right after the owl hoots. Maybe they'll do it again."

We waited, sitting there in the dark. But the owl had apparently said all it intended. And so had Laska. The two had held a brief primeval conversation, out there in the night. No further comment, apparently, was necessary.

Peg was rapidly dropping off to sleep again. I got up and went to the window. Then I gave a howl of my own.

My vocal effort was scarcely equal to the mournful rune that had chilled me a few minutes before. However, a wolf may howl in response to other sounds than those of its own kin—as, indeed, Laska had done at the owl hoot. Auto horns have been answered by wolves in Alaska, just as their domestic counterparts may tune up in response to a fire siren.

Peg and I have visited Algonquin Provincial Park in Ontario. There's a resident wolf pack near the campgrounds. On certain evenings the rangers take campers for a "wolf howl." A caravan goes a short distance from the station. The leader assembles the guests in a quiet circle. Then he raises his voice in a loud "hello-o-o-o."

75

LASKA

He may call again and again with no results. Many evenings are fruitless and the crowd goes home disappointed. But occasionally, off in the forest, there's an answering cry. It's long-drawn, rising and falling with the effect of distance as well as the mood of the shadowy creature that makes it. Rarely, the cry is echoed by another. And another.

The campers shiver a bit, and not merely from the chill. There's something ancient and primitive in the sound of that howl. Most likely it cannot be found in any other human experience. It's a delicious feeling of danger and an uncontrollable thrill.

Wolves used to howl back at the wail of a locomotive as it crossed the western plains. They've answered boat whistles on the Mississippi, and steamers along the Yukon. A few years ago two students went to meditate and play their flutes on a northern hillside. They fled in dismay when a far-off wolf joined their chorus.

Now, with my head out the window, I was trying for the Vermont version of that Algonquin Park. I got results, too—but not what I'd expected. There was a joyous jumping and whining out there in the dark. It sounded a lot more dog than wolf.

And that was that for the call of the wild.

Laska has howled a great deal since. Seldom has it been in the manner of the lonesome cry on that autumn night. Mostly it's an abbreviated call lasting perhaps two seconds. She uses it for greeting where an average dog would bark. It's a quiet howl—companionable, moderately low-pitched. It is not loud or unpleasant at all.

Why do wolves howl? The question has been asked, probably, since the days of the cave dwellers. Steve Greene and I had learned something about it when we visited Isle Royale National Park: they howl for a number of reasons. Nervous energy may prompt one to start, while others may join in for the companionship. The howl serves as a means of keeping the pack together while hunting. The howling of one animal may stir up the rest of the wolves—getting them ready for the trail, perhaps, or merely stretching their legs and vocal cords for a little exercise.

There is another use for the howl. It serves as a substitute for combat. Or, rather, it makes combat unnecessary. Except on rare occasions when they may band together for hunting purposes in winter, wolf packs observe strict territorial lines. When two packs run into each other along the borders there may be an argument. This, in turn, could be foolhardy. It is tough enough to make a living without squandering strength and possibly shedding blood in boundary squabbles. But when two packs howl near each other in the forest, they learn of each other's presence. Then they can part company without ever meeting; and nobody gets hurt.

Laska, of course, had no "pack" but Peg and me. And we've never joined in any hunting expeditions with her. So no matter what the initial purpose of her howl may be, it doubtless ends up as a companionable greeting. Or some sort of comment on her mood of the moment.

One time Jim and Miriam Barlow came to visit. They arrived well after dark in their camper truck. Finding the house unlighted, they figured we had already retired. So they parked the camper and made up their beds for the night.

An hour after they had settled down, we arrived. Our headlights woke them up and soon we were sitting around a midnight snack.

"We didn't know you were running a campground," Miriam said. "Who've you got in the tent?"

"Tent?" I asked. "What tent?"

"Or maybe it's a trailer," Jim added. "At any rate, it's those people camped out there in back of your house. They've been carrying on a conversation ever since we arrived."

Mystified, we went to the door. "There!" said Miriam. "They're still talking."

And she was right. Only it wasn't a tent full of people. It was our chatty canine, discoursing in quiet two-second howls on the events of the past hour and a half.

She'd greeted Jim and Miriam, doubtless, with a little yowl. They probably hadn't heard her as they busied themselves making up the beds. Instead of coming to the door as other visitors did, they merely stayed in the truck. This occasioned a whole string of comments from Laska in her yard. It was her mumbled monologue they'd half heard from within the camper.

❦ ❦ ❦

On Laska's first Christmas a friend brought *Natural
History Magazine*'s album of recorded wolf calls to her.
Narrated by Robert Redford, it contains scores of howls
and growls and barks and whines. There was the hunting
call, for instance. There was the cry of recognition and
the "let's-get-together" call. There was also a social con-
fab of assorted yips and yowls. To us it sounded like an
aimless conversation among a dozen or so wolves—making as much sense as small talk at a cocktail party.

What would Laska do when those wolf howls were
played? We waited until things were quiet and our pup
was asleep on the rug. Then we put the remote speaker
near her and started the record.

First there was the recognition cry. She didn't even
open an eye. The "come-hither" call had the same result. The cocktail party, the hunting calls—no reaction at
all.

Then came the mother and cubs. It's a recording of a
she-wolf entering her den. She calls softly to her young.
The babies answer with hungry little whines. It's a
touching sequence; you can just picture those cubs nuz-
zling the flanks of their mother, there in the dark.

At the first whine of that female, Laska opened her
eyes. A moment later she scrambled to her feet. With
one bound she covered the distance between herself and
the loudspeaker. Another bound took her beyond it; she
wheeled and almost crashed into it. Then, for the rest of
that domestic scene, she sat with her ears forward, eyes
never leaving that speaker.

LASKA

Why the explosive change in her reaction to the record? "No mystery," Peg explained as we considered what had happened. "All those other sounds were grown-up talk. An eight-month-old pup just isn't interested. But when momma comes home with supper— now, that's something else again!"

And I guess she's got the answer.

Laska's hearing is incredibly keen. One winter day when the snow lay deep, I was walking with her down the driveway. She pranced ahead of me, tail waving. Suddenly, with only the briefest pause to take aim, she gave a great leap into a snowdrift. It was such a smooth motion that I was caught off guard—as was the unfortunate shrew that apparently had squeaked just at the wrong time.

The quality of a sound is important, too. The right tone or pitch brings a startling result. One time after our pet was full grown, a stranger drove up in his little foreign car. I'd let Laska run a few minutes while I was working in the garden. I heard the car on the driveway and rushed to put in the last transplant before going to meet my visitor.

As I came around the corner, trowel in hand, I saw that Laska had arrived ahead of me. She joyfully bounded up to the car, tail wagging.

The driver had busied himself getting something from the back seat. When he turned around again she stood there, eyes level with his and just inches away. All eighty pounds of her.

He spoke a cautious word of greeting as he started to open the door. Something in his voice must have sounded like an owl, perhaps, or a boat whistle. Pointing that white muzzle skyward, she serenaded the visitor. Both barrels, full cry, all stops out.

The door closed. The window hastily went up. Man and beast looked at each other through a pane of glass.

That tail was still wagging, however. He decided to chance it. I saw the window go down about three inches. "Nice doggie?" he asked.

Obviously he wasn't sure what the answer might be. So I ambled out of the bushes and to the rescue. Laska came running and the gentleman opened the door once more.

"Friendly, huh?" he ventured, with a wary eye on our exuberant greeting committee.

"Oh sure—" I began.

Laska finished my sentence with a fine, doleful moan.

Our visitor was more out of the car than in. The door closed weakly behind him. He stood there, flattened against the automobile as if before a firing squad.

"—friendly as a kitten," I concluded.

But he scarcely looked reassured. He'd never met a dog like this before. Certainly not one as musical. I didn't know why his speech produced such an effect on her vocal cords, but apparently his voice was tuned to Laska's wavelength. Even if the rest of him wasn't.

I was about to collar Laska when she solved the problem all by herself. The nose went skyward again, but this time no howl. Sitting down in the grass she closed her eyes, took careful aim with the toes of one hind foot— and industriously scratched a flea.

No wolf about to devour you will take time out for a flea, and our visitor knew it. He grinned and relaxed. "I'm Tom Arnold," he said. Then, indicating the now-reclining Laska, "Interesting pet you got there."

I introduced myself and Laska. It turned out that our visitor was a member of a small religious group. His mission was to visit every home in the community. We had a fine chat. By the time we were through, he and Laska were good friends.

He got into the car and started the engine. "That dog is the greatest talker I ever saw."

"Yep," I agreed. "She's a conversationalist all right. I wonder what she was saying when you first arrived?"

"Don't know," he said. "But for a while I was afraid it might be grace before meals."

Another example of Laska's "wavelength" occurred when we paid a visit to Hilltop House. Hilltop House is a retirement home in Brattleboro, with about two dozen residents. Marion Looman, the administrator, had asked if I'd be able to give a slidetalk there. So, late one afternoon on my way through southern Vermont, I material-ized at the home with projector, slides, and Laska. She was to go with me on a visit to my folks in Connecticut.

The visit was a success, at least Laska's part of it. She

seemed to sense the frailty of the older people around her, and stood patiently to be petted, rather than darting from one person to another as she usually did in a crowd. Apparently the solid feel of her large, thick-furred body was comforting to her admirers; there were several hands on her at once.

The slides, alas, did not fare so well. I'd forgotten the limitations of tired old eyes. After hearing a murmured "what's that?" several times from the audience, I realized that the pictures might be little more than blurs of colors on the screen. So I tried to describe each as best I could.

Meantime, Laska, aided and abetted by two dozen elderly persons hungry for affection, constantly upstaged my best photographic efforts and my most captivating line of patter. No matter. It was their evening, not mine. Indeed, I was as delighted as they were. And when the residents of Hilltop House insisted we stay the night, I felt that glow of warmth that comes from helping make others happy.

I called my own aging parents and told them not to expect me until around noon the next day. Then, since "lights out" comes early in a retirement home, I retired to the guest room with a glass of milk, a few fresh-baked cookies and my wolfdog.

We had breakfast together the next morning. It was Laska's first order of eggs sunny-side-up. With bacon, too—even if it all went down in less time and with less ceremony than it took most of us with our own portions.

Our leave taking turned out to be a howling success. Literally. As I stood at the door, Marion Looman asked if our wolfdog made any noise. Until now, Laska had been completely silent. So I decided I'd try to oblige them and persuade Laska to perform. "Wolf call!" I said. "Let's hear it!"

I gave a little howl to get her started, but there was no answer. I tried again and again. "Guess she's not in the mood," I explained. "Maybe next time—"

At this moment one of Laska's new friends decided to give it a try. A woman supported by a walker took a good hitch on what once must have been a stalwart pair of lungs. "Ow-o-o-o!" she cried in a voice that could have been heard on the third floor.

The wolfdog turned to look at her. She braced those white paws. Up went the snout. And Laska, the blue-eyed wolfdog, serenaded Hilltop House and half of Brattleboro with a fine, full-throated howl.

CHAPTER

VIII

A CAR CAME TO A STOP on the road down by our wooden bridge. I waited for the planks to rumble as the vehicle drove across, but they made not a sound. Our fifty-foot doorbell, as Peg calls the creaky structure, was silent.

Perhaps the driver was getting out to clean the windshield or make some minor adjustment. Possibly the car was merely turning around and would go the other way in a moment. Maybe it was an angler about to try for a trout in the river under the bridge. In any case, the car merely stayed there, engine idling.

Cars stop along our road every day. Bird watchers, anglers, picnickers—all find something of interest on that straight stretch between Lewie Cloe's house and the foot of Page Hill a quarter mile away. There's one difference between them and this car, however: they turn their engines off.

Ordinarily I'd have not given that car a further thought, but there was some indefinable importance to it. Indeed, something almost ominous. It was as if our bridge and our property were quietly being watched.

Ten minutes passed. Then the car started up. The bridge rumbled its greeting—or warning—and there was the sound of tires on the gravel. The engine labored up the little hill and around the curve, then slacked off as the driveway straightened out.

We were about to have company.

I sauntered out to meet the car. If my misgivings were correct, we could talk out there in the summer air. And if my suspicions were unfounded, I could invite my visitor in for a chat.

One look was all I needed. From the driver's side of the car emerged a man in a uniform. Stepping out from the door on the other side was an unsmiling gentleman who looked as if he just had eaten something sour.

Peg and I have always enjoyed warm and friendly relations with our game wardens. In the process of sheltering and rehabilitating scores of wild animals through the years, we've often had occasion to enlist their help. As such creatures are usually subject to state and federal controls, we've always checked with the warden before taking in an unfortunate animal temporarily down on its luck.

Our property is admirably suited to such events. We can see no human neighbor in any direction. Beyond our patches of open fields and overgrown pasture are thousands of acres of Green Mountain National Forest. Thus a wounded squirrel or an orphaned raccoon can probably find something to its liking when returning health and self-reliance call it to leave our hospitality.

People often wonder how we can hold on to such creatures until time for their departure. But the problem is seldom that of keeping them. Rather, it's persuading them to leave. It's as if this free meal ticket was preferable to life among unexpected dangers in an unknown land. So, in caring for more than three hundred wild animals, we've seldom had the need for a cage.

In fact, a cage would be breaking the law. "You can have all the wild creatures you wish wandering free on your land," Warden Ed Strobridge once told me. "On your lawn and in your trees and in your garden, for that matter. But once you start penning them—even for their own protection—that's when the officials get nervous."

We were caring for no wild animals, penned or unpenned, at the moment. Nor had we had any in the past several weeks. So that couldn't be the reason for the visit.

"Good morning, Ron," the warden said. "Guess you and Bill have met."

I nodded, then waited.

"Nice day," the warden offered.

"Yep," I said. "Had several of them lately."

"Ron—do you have a dog?"

Oh-oh. The warden already knew I had a dog. And so, I was sure, did his companion. "Sure, Sam. She's the same one I've had for more than a year now. I guess you met her last winter when you brought me that opossum you found in Rutland—"

But he wouldn't be sidetracked. "She's the one that's half wolf?"

"Quarter wolf. Her mother's half wolf. The father's Siberian husky. So that makes her quarter wolf."

The other man coughed. Sam glanced in his direction. "Wonder if Bill and I could see her for a minute, Ron?"

"Sure. She's in her yard. Out by the corner of the house."

They fell in behind me as I led the way out to Laska's pen. Perhaps confining a quarter wolf was somehow illegal, even though John Trotier had assured me there'd be no trouble when he sold her to me.

Laska was perched atop her doghouse. Seeing our delegation she welcomed us with a friendly howl. Then she jumped down and came bounding to the gate. Those white paws drummed the earth; the long bushy tail with its white underside waved like a plume.

Bill spoke. "She's your only dog?"

I nodded. "Why—is something wrong?"

Bill looked perplexed. "No. No—I guess there isn't."

Then Sam explained. "We've been getting word of a band of dogs attacking farm animals between here and Ripton. Bill got a glimpse of them yesterday. One of them looked as if it might be Laska."

❋ ❋ ❋

My mind raced back to the events of the past twenty-four hours. Had Laska been safely in her yard? Could I prove it? Or had the door been left ajar? Had she somehow sneaked out when nobody was looking—and then sneaked back in again?

But I needn't have worried. Bill spoke up and saved me. "Well," he said slowly, "I thought it might be your dog. That is, until I see her close up. That other dog was a husky breed, like yours. But yours doesn't have the right kind of a tail."

I gazed at Laska's nether appendage. Unlike the average husky tail that curls up over the back, it stood straight out to the rear. Indeed, except for being black and white instead of brown with dark hairs along its upper side, it was a typical wolf tail.

As with her wild forbears, when Laska was in high spirits the tail waved aloft. As her enthusiasm waned the tail progressively drooped. Thus it was a furry barometer of her attitude toward life. And now, little aware of the solemnity with which we regarded her, she pranced back and forth—tail hoisted like a flag.

We contemplated her a few minutes more. "Don't worry about the mistaken identity," I told the two. "It's great to know she's in the clear."

And so she was—for about two weeks. The husky in her had been brought to trial and acquitted. Soon it was the turn of the wolf.

Actually, the wolf was on trial much of the time. Peo-

ple who didn't know of Laska's parentage would give her
a friendly pat. They'd look into those startling blue husky
eyes and, like as not, receive a dry lick from a warm pink
tongue. Then, for some undefinable reason, they'd
pause.

Perhaps it was the long, slender legs. Perhaps it was
that expressive, bushy tail. Possibly it was her little howl
of greeting when they first met her. Or perhaps it was
some inborn wariness that still lurks in us from the days
of the spear and the fire and the club. But somewhere
after that pause would be the inevitable question: "She's
a husky, all right—but what else?"

People who met her in this way usually accepted her
easily. They could hardly do otherwise; she was the soul
of friendliness—a trait of both the husky and the wolf.
When they parted company the comment was nearly
always the same: "I can believe she is part wolf."

It wasn't those who met her that caused the problem.
It was those who hadn't. Including the woman who cornered me at the supermarket. My shopping cart was
nearly filled and I'd gone back for a last item when I
spotted her bearing down on me.

Somehow I knew there'd be trouble. I careened
around the corner, intending to escape down the next
aisle. But she anticipated my move and headed me off.
"Oh, *there* you are, Mr. Rood," she said. "I've been hoping to catch up with you."

Then, she got right to the point. "Mr. Rood, what is

it that you have up there in Lincoln? What kind of an animal?"

"Well, Peg and I don't have many animals these days. We're both traveling a lot, and I give lectures all over the country. So about all we have is an aquarium. And a dog."

This, I knew, was the opening she wanted. "What kind of dog?"

"Part Siberian husky." Then, since she was expecting it anyway, I gave her the rest "—and part timber wolf."

"You mean you've got a wolf right there at your house?"

"Sure. Had her more than a year now. Come up and meet her some time. She loves company—any kind."

"And do you let her run around loose?"

Enough. A few idle words in the store was one thing; the third degree was another. Obviously the woman had a bone to pick. And I wasn't about to have that bone be me. "Only," I said, "on the full of the moon."

She gave me a withering look. "Mr. Rood, I am *not* joking. My grandchildren live on the road near your house. They are apt to be out at any time on their bicycles. I will not have them exposed to a wolf."

Here I was confronted with that old, old prejudice against wolves. Since the woman hadn't ever met Laska she suspected the worst. And little I could say would change her mind. So I decided to give her the truth and let it go at that.

LASKA

"The 'wolf' you refer to," I told her, "has a mother on one of the most famous sled teams in Vermont. She and her mother have been petted and loved by all kinds of people from kids to grandparents. She has been a guest of honor at a retirement home. If you'd let her, she would be a guest at your home as well."

The woman opened her mouth to speak, but I was wound up. "In the meantime," I said, "be assured she is safely in a special yard we made for her. Never will I let any wolf of mine eat even a single one of your grand-children."

We have had other reactions to Laska. In spite of my assurances that Laska has no designs on anything larger than a chunk of liver or a hambone, people take no chances. She's part wolf and they don't forget it. When they drive into the yard they "accidentally" honk the horn, just to let us know they've arrived. Parents often leave their children in the car and gingerly make their way toward the house. One traveling salesman ran half-way out to where I was mowing the lawn and then ran back for a forgotten sample case—all the while keeping an eye on Laska's yard. Apparently seeing her behind a fence wasn't enough. He must have figured she'd choose that moment to break out.

Then there's the problem of stray dogs. The pack that had been molesting farm animals was finally broken up, by the way, when two were hit by a single car. One was the husky that had been mistaken for Laska. The other was a silky-haired creature that seemed to be part Irish setter. Both animals looked well fed and well loved. Each had a collar and I.D. tag. Their owners were flabbergasted when told of the tragedy that had occurred more than a mile from home. Which, I guess, points out there's a bit of the wanderer in even the most pampered pet.

We figured Laska probably had her share of wanderlust, too. After all, wolves have been known to travel as much as forty miles in a day and a night. So her fence was to protect not only our own wildlife but the creatures beyond our borders as well.

The fence was especially important in winter. One of the problems of those bleak days is that a crust or packed layer will sometimes form on the deep snow. This layer is not strong enough to hold up a deer, but will support the weight of a dog. Hence the family pooch may go exploring with another dog, come across the trail of a deer—and there's the start of an unfair and unequal race. The deer flounders along, breaking through the snow while the dogs run easily on top. Even if they do not catch the distraught creature, they may run it to exhaustion. And this is at a time when it needs all its energy just to stay alive.

Now and again the baying of dogs after deer may be heard by one of my neighbors. The next day, perhaps, when I'm in the Lincoln Country Store I learn about it. "The dogs are running the deer again," someone will say.

There'll be a silence. Then comes the apparently

unrelated question: "How's your dog these days, Ron? The one that's part wolf?"

Or we may get a telephone call. It's almost always in an apologetic tone, as our neighbors are our friends. Yet a dog—any dog—is an unknown quantity when it's not under control. So, after a few comments about the weather and how's everything anyway, my caller comes to the point.

"Woods are awful dry, Ron (or wet, or green, or snowy)."

"Yep; never saw them drier (or wetter, or greener, or snowier)."

"My boy saw a couple dogs through the trees an hour ago. Didn't get a good look, but just wondered if yours might of busted loose."

"Gosh, thanks for thinking of us. But she's in her yard. Been there all morning."

"Oh, fine. Just thought I'd check."

"Sure. I appreciate the call."

We hang up. I go out and thoughtfully stroke that thick fur. Or perhaps I just stand and contemplate our canine White Elephant. Black and white, to be exact— with a little brown on the hips and hocks where the wolf shows through.

"You're a good girl," I tell her. "But good for *what*, I haven't figured out yet."

So, over the years, our wolfdog has affected people in a number of ways. They've ranged from simple disbelief through amusement to a despairing look that indicates we must have taken leave of our senses.

The same was true of the reaction to Laska's mother. John Trotier told me Wolf has collected all of these responses.

And more, unfortunately, as I found out one day when I visited John. "How is that lead dog of yours doing?" I asked. "Any more puppies?"

He gave me an odd look, but didn't answer. Then there was a little sound as if he'd caught his breath. I glanced up quickly. His eyes were brimming with tears.

"She—she's no more, Ron."

The last time I had seen Wolf she had been very much alive, playful, expansive: tail waving just as Laska's did, white feet dancing with the expectation of a good run. What on earth had happened?

I didn't have long to wait for the answer. Hesitantly at first as he searched for the words, and then in a torrent, John told the tragic story. He'd taken his team up into Quebec for a race. There were all kinds of dogs in the competition—malemutes, huskies, Samoyeds, and nondescript mongrels. There was also Wolf and her Siberian running mates.

As usual, people were fascinated by the lanky lead dog. They asked the usual questions, John said—whether she'd turn wild or cross as she got older; whether she fought with the other dogs; whether he dared turn his back on her; how she'd behave if she ever got away.

95

He responded just as he had so many times before, assuring them that most of those notions were in their heads—not hers. "And as far as I knew, I'd answered all their questions, Ron, so everybody was happy."

It was a three-day event. John Trotier's team put on a splendid showing. Spectators, photographers, even opposing drivers were impressed by the great, ground-gobbling strides of this powerful wolfdog and her team-mates.

It was the morning of the last day. John went out to the dozen or so boxes on a trailer body that served as a mobile home for his charges. There was an outburst of yelps and whines as the dogs chorused their eagerness to be on the trail again.

But one box was silent. Alarmed, John opened the clasp that fastened Wolf's door. There was no dry-tongued lick to the hand he thrust inside. All he felt was a solid, unyielding mass of fur. There was no motion—not even any warmth.

Numbly, he pulled her body out to where he could look at her. Numbly he accepted someone's offer to get the show's veterinarian. While the other teams took their places and raced away and out of sight, he heard the veterinarian's diagnosis:

Wolf had been poisoned.

His spectacular lead dog, the half wolf who'd made her entire living with dogs and sleds and the adulation of thousands of persons over half a continent, was dead.

"And why?" John asked, his words trembling with agony, "Why? Was it because somebody had a grudge against me? Did somebody have a grudge against my dogs?"

He sat down a moment, then got up and paced the floor. "Or—" his voice rose to a shout—"was it greed? Did somebody else want the prize money? Was someone going to lose a bet if we won?"

He collapsed in a chair. Then he leaned forward until his face was just inches from mine. "Or did it go deeper than that?" he asked quietly. "I've seen it out in the open sometimes; other times it's hiding. But I can feel it's there. Did they kill her not because of *who* she was, but *what* she was—because she was one-half wolf?"

He looked at me, pleading for an answer. But I could say nothing. The only one with an adequate reply was the person who'd done the deed. And, perhaps, not even that person could really give the answer. Fear and hate can upset reason and judgment.

I comforted my friend as best I could. There was little sense in saying there'd be other dogs and other races; nothing would replace his valued Wolf. "But," he said, after a few minutes, "I'm building the team up as best I can."

Then he brightened. "Want to take a look?"

So we went out to his yard and tried to put the tragic event behind us. For half an hour we chatted and petted the dogs. I admired his latest sled and some changes

97

he'd made on the trailer. Then we parted company, with no mention of the empty kennel, the chain that lay slack under the trees. . . .

Back home, I was greeted by a friendly howl and the sound of paws at that gate out beyond the corner of the house. I let my own wolfdog out of her yard. Then I knelt down and looked into the depths of those blue eyes.

"Laska," I said, "perhaps your mother *was* killed because she was part wolf. But in this little town, you're among friends. Nothing like that would ever happen here."

But I said it with a heartiness I didn't quite feel. And later I was to understand why.

CHAPTER

IX

PEG CAME IN, stamping the snow off her feet. "Looks as if something had a convention out there last night."

I followed her into the yard. There were fresh tracks from the corner of the garage to the back door. They led out to Laska's pen. They went along the perimeter of the fence and past the closed gate. The tracks circled the fence several times, then crisscrossed the yard.

"A little dog," I told Peg. "Or maybe a couple of them."

I looked more carefully at the tracks. Where they went over to a small bush they were in perfect single file. No domestic canine walked so precisely. "Correction," I said. "Let's say those tracks were made by a fox."

Dogs, it seems, often make a separate track with each of their four feet. Foxes usually walk with each hind foot fitting exactly in the print of a forefoot. The result is a long line of tracks, one behind the other, as if made by a creature with just one leg.

LASKA

Laska had been in the house overnight. Apparently she'd not been aware of the visit of her thick-furred little cousin. Or, if she heard or smelled it, she hadn't made enough noise to wake us.

Red foxes are not uncommon in the woods and fields of our old farm. They usually give our yard a wide berth, however, or travel across the lawn without stopping. Last night's unusual behavior must have a special meaning. Bundling up against the chill of that early March morning, I went out to investigate.

After its inspection of the premises, the fox had headed off down the driveway. There, on a clod of snow, it had left its calling card: a musky little pat of fecal material. Then it headed off into the woods. I followed the trail a short distance further. It went up toward the ledges. Apparently surprising a snowshoe hare beneath a snow-draped hemlock, the fox had sprinted away through the evergreens.

The snow was too heavy on those coniferous branches to allow me to go any farther. At every step I got a fresh load dumped down my neck. So I turned back toward the house, still wondering about the fox's antics in our yard.

In answer to my wife's inquiring look, I shrugged. "Must've been just curious, Peg."

She smiled. "And apparently it's catching. Look out by the blueberries."

I had set out half a dozen blueberry plants in front of

✹　✹　✹

the house. Now one of them was being investigated by
somebody's dog. Fluffy-headed, frizzle-haired, it was
brown and black and every other color a dog has been
known to be. A surprisingly long tail waved back and
forth as the creature sniffed the bush from all sides. It
lifted its leg, dog fashion, against the bush. As it did so, it
looked up toward the house. We were in plain sight,
standing at the window. The dog paused, as it were, in
midair. Then, with a startled "Woof!" it ran off down the
driveway. Partway down the hill it stopped.

As we gazed at that fleeing apparition, the thought
hit us both at once. We turned and looked at our sleeping pup, there on the rug. "Why, Laska!" Peg said. "You
mean you're growing up?"

And growing up she was, indeed. In a couple of
weeks she'd celebrate her second birthday. And undoubtedly she'd given word of her maturity in the little
urine scent-posts she'd established up and down the
driveway and around the yard.

Laska was coming into heat.

Cautioning Peg to keep the doors closed, I took another walk down the driveway. This time I looked closer.
Here and there our pup had left telltale drops of blood
against the snow. That fox—undoubtedly a male—and
the nondescript vagabond canine had been quick to pick
up the scent.

The fox, of course, could never be her mate. Probably, as I had suggested to Peg, it was merely curious.

LASKA

The multi-colored dog, however, was motivated by more than curiosity. For the next two weeks, more or less, he might be in constant attendance around our most attractive yard.

This would be the end of Laska's morning romps. At least for awhile. I was glad we lived a few hundred feet from the road, as stray dogs traveled along it every day. No telling what kind of hopeful suitors Laska would have if we lived right on the highway.

We hadn't discussed the possibility of her having puppies. After all, up to now she had been only a puppy herself. Now we had to make a decision. But neither of us wanted to make it this fast. So while we considered the situation she'd have to go into retirement.

Merely placing her in her yard with the gate firmly locked wouldn't do it. That shaggy dog would be back, we knew. His attentions, even though thwarted by the fence, would doubtless become decidedly vocal. Besides, if a dog and a fox had found the way, no telling who'd be next.

She'd have to stay in the house with us. With just the two of us there, we could keep an eye on her as we went in and out the door. In fact, we'd better keep the doors locked. Many of our Vermont neighbors have the habit of just giving a perfunctory knock and entering before we've had a chance to respond. I could just see eighty pounds of amorous Whatsis bowling somebody over in her anxiety to get to the outside world and the nearest lucky swain.

So we put Laska under house arrest. Then, morning and night, I figured, I could take her out on a strong leash to her yard. Letting her romp and relieve herself in the yard, I'd be able to watch her until it was time to take her in again. In this way the three of us could survive that two weeks with scant attention from the rest of the world.

Which goes to show how little we really understood about canine nature. For her part, Laska accepted the confinement in good grace, but that was only half the story. The other half lay in the surprising sensibilities of the rest of dogdom Out There.

Of course the mop-headed pooch was back in an hour that first morning. You don't shoo a dog away at such times by merely gazing at him through the window. This time he had reinforcement, if you could call it that, in the person of a diminutive but optimistic little white terrier. This hopeful creature could probably walk right under Laska's stomach without having to stoop at all.

They gave the yard a thorough going over. They investigated the fox trail and followed it down the driveway. Where the fox had left his souvenir they soberly added their own signatures. Then they disappeared down toward the road—the big dog in the lead, the little white one waddling along behind.

And so we started our two-week vigil. Each time one of us would leave the house, the other would dutifully lock the door. Laska could no longer frisk along with us as we went down to get the mail at the bottom of the hill or put in half an hour with the snow shovel. She must have been puzzled by the elaborate ritual every time we went in or out.

But it worked. Or, at least, part way. We kept Laska safe—if "safe" would be the word she'd use if she could talk. However, our yard turned into a dog show. That pen where she exercised twice daily was of surpassing interest. A friendly beagle sniffed all around it one morning, along with somebody's Irish setter. A coonhound, finding few raccoons this time of year, arrived to while away the time.

There were several other less identifiable dogs as well—from that faithful many-colored mutt to an interesting canine who had the general look of a German shepherd but was spotted like a Dalmatian.

"Wonder what a cross between that dog and Laska would look like?" I asked as we contemplated the unlikely creature.

Bill Givens, a friend, was with us at the time. "Might be a good experiment," he said. "The pups would make great fire dogs, being part Dalmatian. And with the wolf howl you'd have a built-in siren."

Peg decided it might go the other way. "You'd probably end up with a spotted wolf that sat around all day and barked."

Then there was the big black Lab. He was a friendly fellow—a purebred Labrador retriever, from the looks, with a red collar. I noted the number on his dog tags and found out where he lived from Calvin Darling, our town clerk.

He was too nice a dog to have running loose anyway, so I called his owners. They were flabbergasted that their well-bred pet was cavorting like a common cur. Piling him into their car, they assured me I'd never see him again.

Well, that was the end of him. The days passed and there was no sign of him. Obviously they were as good as their word.

Then, one morning I was sitting at the typewriter in my study. Peg had gone off to her kindergarten classes at school, and there was just Laska and me, locked in the house. She'd been "in season" for more than a week now and, except for those hopeful dogs out in the yard, things were going well.

All at once there was a commotion in the other room. Laska let out a howl. There was an odd noise, with the sound of glass in it. She came racing into the study, whirled and dashed back out again.

I followed her as fast as I could. I was just in time to see her fling herself at our big picture window. Her eighty pounds, propelled by doggy ardor, might well have buckled the glass except for one little detail: there was something on the other side that cancelled the blow.

That something was a big, black Lab. He was standing full height, beating against the window with his paws.

LASKA

Laska got to her feet after the crash. Then, in spite of my shout of dismay, she, too, began to paw at the window.

A total of perhaps a hundred fifty pounds of determination thumped against our precious picture window from two sides. I raced forward, grabbed Laska by the collar, and marched her into another part of the house. Then, dashing outside, I yelled at the startled Labrador. He disappeared amidst a rain of snowballs.

No. Locked doors weren't good enough. Those dogs would go through the window if they got half a chance. I wouldn't have been surprised to see one come down the chimney. We'd have to put up another barrier.

And so Laska was relegated to the cellar. At first she acted as if puzzled at this odd turn of events, but her good nature soon came through. Especially when I pulled the old rug out of her doghouse and put it on the cellar floor. Then, to soften the blow further, I got a handful of bones from the Bristol Market and gave her a fresh snack every time we put her down in her dungeon.

We managed to scrape up enough soil from a nearby gravel bank so she'd visit it like a cat with a litter box. And there she stayed for her last week.

One day our daughter, Janice, brought her little black male dog with her on a visit. Duffy lived in the old farmhouse down at the bottom of our driveway with Jan, her husband Steve, and their daughter, Jenny. They'd carefully kept him inside. Except for one or two escapes he'd remained in wishful seclusion. Now, this time, he'd been allowed to ride up the hill "as long as you stay in the car, Duffy."

Duffy, however, managed to tumble out as Jennifer opened the car door. He bounded ahead of them and was waiting when they got to the house. "Guess I'd better put him back in the car?" Janice suggested.

Two weeks and two days had passed since that first visit by the fox. Perhaps Duffy would be a good trial balloon, so to speak. We needed some way to know when Laska was no longer receptive to the opposite sex.

We were all tired of the cellar routine, anyway. "Let him in, Jan," I told her. "I'll bring Laska up from the cellar. Perhaps things are okay by now."

Laska and Duffy had long been good friends. Now, as we watched, she came prancing up the cellar stairs. Duffy, no doubt overwhelmed by the immense possibility of having her to himself at last, rushed to meet her.

He's a little dog, scarcely half her bulk. But size matters not to male or female when romance is concerned. Valiantly he tried to throw an arm around her.

With a roar, she whirled on him. Teeth flashing, she knocked him to the floor. Duffy let out a yowl, did a half-gainer, and scuttled out of the way.

And that was that. Laska's ordeal—plus that of her friends, human and animal—was over. She could run the driveway once more, and sleep in her yard. And, if we needed further proof that she was her old self again, that canine assemblage suddenly vanished.

Things were back to normal. Normal for another

year, perhaps, if the wolf in her was calling the play. The female wolf's breeding season takes place once a year. But if the Siberian husky was setting the scene, we'd have the problem to face again in another six months.

Then what would we do? Mate her with that tortoise-shell hobo who'd been so much in evidence the entire two weeks? The Dalmatian? That black Lab?

Or, since her mother was no longer alive, should we breed Laska to one of John Trotier's Siberians to help him compensate for his loss?

Then, too, there was another possibility. How about taking her to the Canadian outpost where her grand-mother had been born—where Laska could meet one of her wild wolf relatives the next time she came in heat?

It was an intriguing thought. But only for a moment. Laska was enough wolf, thanks. Any such Canadian imports would be breaking our own rule about not keeping wild animals.

Besides, the minute we got puppies of any kind we'd have to determine what to do with them. And, as Peg reminded me, we were losing sight of why we got Laska in the first place. Certainly it wasn't to put us in the dog business.

So we had to decide on the step that would deprive her forever of the chance to have a family. A routine spaying procedure by a veterinarian would do it in a few minutes. She'd be at the infirmary just a day or two; then she'd be back with us. Simple as that.

It was an agonizing decision, and it took weeks to make. We considered the reasons our wolfdog should have all her normal faculties, and why she should be allowed to retain her womanhood. But we kept coming back to the undeniable fact: one part wolf around the place was enough.

In fact, more than enough, when we considered the peril to the picture window, the two-week vigil by Laska's gentleman friends, and the job it had been to clean the cellar when things were back to normal.

Hence, one spring day when Peg headed for her school in Middlebury, Laska went with her. Peg left her off at Dr. Greiner's Animal Hospital and picked her up again two days later.

And there she was, back with us, with the wolf locked inside her forever. In a few days she was as bouncy as before. She paid little attention to that neatly healing incision on her abdomen. There was apparently not one shred of change in our frisky pup.

Yet I couldn't help feeling I'd betrayed her. "But I'll make it up to you somehow," I said, as she gazed at me with those blue eyes, unaware of the dramatic difference those few days had wrought,"—I promise."

CHAPTER

X

NOWHERE, PROBABLY, has the wolf been more respected than in the mind of the American Indian. The Indian, of course, knew the great creature well and was much impressed by its strength and intelligence.

Often, before taking the life of a wolf, a hunter would breathe a quiet prayer to its spirit. In this prayer he explained how he needed the wolf skin for warmth, its fur as an edging for his parka, its teeth and paws as talismans that held great power.

Barry Lopez, in his book *Of Wolves and Men*, points out the Indian's feeling for this creature. The Ceremony of the Wolf was a solemn occasion, lasting several days. Some braves wore wolf skins into combat. Some carried tails or paws or bits of fur for bravery and skill and protection from harm. To be a member of the Wolf Clan made you an important person, indeed.

Now that we have had our own version of that wilderness creature, we can understand a little of the Indian's point of view. Of course Laska's actions are scarcely those of a wild animal. Then, too, she's mostly Siberian husky—one of the oldest domestic breeds on earth. Yet there's enough of the primitive in her to give us an occasional fleeting glimpse of the timber wolf.

The way she engages in combat, for instance—even when it's only in play—is much like the tactics of her wild relatives. A big, friendly golden retriever named Joe occasionally pays us a visit. If I let Laska out for a few minutes of recreation with him they're soon engaged in a whirlwind battle.

Actually it's whirlwind only on Laska's part. Joe, with good nature, bears the brunt of an attack from everywhere at once. Leaping, dancing, sometimes vaulting completely over her "foe," Laska darts at him and bounds away again almost before he can respond. Again and again she jumps at him, jaws snapping with each near miss.

She swarms over him, seldom actually touching him, but mounting such a devastating blitz that sometimes his patience deserts him. With a roar of exasperation he lunges at her—but of course, she is not there. He whirls a few more times, lets out a frustrated "you don't play fair!"—and, somehow, talks her into a more conventional tussle.

I have never actually seen a wild wolf in battle, but motion pictures show much the same bewildering onslaught when the great creatures are in a fight. George

Miksch Sutton, in his celebrated book *High Arctic*, tells
of an attack by a hungry wolf on a single bull muskox.
Sutton and his companions had often seen the bull near
their camp. Then, one day, a member of their party saw
the end:

"Dave Gray gave us a blow-by-blow account of the
killing of the bull muskox . . . The muskox was by himself when the wolf approached. At first Dave thought the
wolf was merely teasing or employing 'diversionary
tactics,' waiting for another wolf, or several wolves, to ap-
pear. But what looked like frolic and romping was anything but that: it was lethal tactics. There was no nipping
at hindquarters, no attempt to hamstring. Every attack
was directed at the head. The muskox swung fiercely
with his horns; but the wolf—nimble, powerful,
expert—danced about, waiting for an opening. Surprising his quarry with a sudden lunge, the wolf got past the
horns and tore off hair and an eye. The muskox continued to toss his great head, doing his best to gore his
assailant; but loss of blood and eye told on him. Finally
the wolf seized the throat, and the muskox went down.
The battle had lasted 53 minutes—from 8:20 to 9:13
p.m. Before leaving his kill, the wolf tore away great
mouthfuls of hair, broke the ribs behind one shoulder
blade, drank blood, and ate the tongue."

Yet its strength and sagacity and nimbleness are but
devices that enable the wolf to gain its food and to stay
alive. As Robert Redford points out in the *Natural His-*

***

tory Magazine record that excited Laska as a puppy, the wolf has no more personal animosity toward its prey than we do in attacking a sirloin steak or in picking an apple off a tree.

Thus the friendliness that is so much a part of Laska's make-up should not be so surprising. It could easily come from the dog in her. The husky has been, quite literally, in the bosom of the family of the northern Indian and Eskimo. There it served as a source, not only of transportation, but of comfort. It was not unusual for a sled dog to sleep right with the family—and thus everybody kept warm.

So it's natural to be sociable, as far as the husky in Laska is concerned. The wolf in her makes it even more so. After all, the wolf is a pack animal. When they are together, wolves lick and rub against each other, tails waving in high good spirits. When one or two members of the pack return after an absence, the rest of the animals rise to greet them. For a few minutes there is a general good-natured reunion all around.

It's not sociability itself that shows us the wolf in Laska; it's what happens next. Come into the house, for instance, where she has been snoozing on the floor. She'll get up and greet you joyously with that dry-tongued lick—another wolflike trait. Then she'll go back to her slumbers.

And here, I believe, is where her wild ancestry shows. For, no matter how delirious she seems at your arrival, she'll lie down in a certain way. That way is to position herself so she's facing you. It is nothing personal, I am sure. It's just that somewhere beneath that exuberance is an age-old message, handed down for eons:

Here's someone new. Take care. Never turn your back on a stranger.

Another quirk that may come from those generations in the wilderness is the way Laska chases a ball. Throw the ball along a smooth surface—a driveway, say, or a close-clipped lawn—so it has plenty of speed. Doglike, Laska goes after it. But when she catches up to it, something interesting happens. Instead of pouncing on it, she races in front—as if to head it off.

I've seen movies of wolves trying to capture a moose. While most of the pack brings up the rear, one or two run ahead to slow it from the front. This, I believe, is the point of Laska's action: she's heading that ball off so that the rest of her "pack"—Peg and I— can catch it from behind.

It's hard, of course, to take any one trait of behavior and announce "that's what a dog would do," or "that shows the wolf in her."

"Good heavens," Peg said one day as we were trying to figure out where the dog stopped and the wolf began, "we can't even explain our own actions. How's anybody going to psychoanalyze Laska?"

Yet we keep having that feeling of being in the presence of something besides a dog. There's a certain way she reacts to a situation, for instance, or something she does on her own.

Most dogs show little concern about mirrors. Although their eyes tell them "yes," their nose and ears say "no," and they turn away. Laska, however, has been interested in mirrors since her first startled "woof!" at one when she was a puppy.

Perhaps, we figure, the wolf running headlong through the woods with the pack depends more on sight than does the dog, whose vision has lost its keenness over centuries of domestication. Thus the image of another creature in a mirror deserves at least further investigation.

Of course some dogs follow their eyes, too—the greyhound, for instance, and the retriever. But another of Laska's pecularities startles me every time it occurs: if I stare fixedly at some object she'll turn and look in that direction, too.

I have long puzzled over this trait. It's an interesting bit of behavior. Dogs are often alert to every change in your facial expression, true. But a dog will seldom follow your gaze.

Is it because Laska is part of a pack when she's with us? As the "alpha wolf," does my abiding interest in something mean she should be interested too? Have I spotted an elk or a caribou? Should she make certain that she also sees it so as to help in the hunt?

LASKA

It's a temptation to endow animals with human thoughts and feelings. At one time anybody who entertained such notions was practically drummed out of biology class. Now, with those strides in our communication with apes and dolphins, it's not quite such an open-and-shut case. Especially when you realize those people who considered animals as living robots often based their views on captive or laboratory specimens. And some laboratory conditions can be pretty harrowing.

So Laska, Peg, and I are the three members of our wolfdog's "pack." The way it is arranged, I suppose, is that I am the boss, or "alpha wolf" with Peg second-in-command and with Laska down the scale somewhere.

She's a pack member, yes, with the sense of security that must go along with it. But there's another trait that may have been passed down unchanged from her wild ancestors. It is an odd contrast to the predatory nature that will send that pack twenty miles after a moose or caribou: a sudden loss of courage. A wolf that will face an enraged bison may shy away from a butterfly.

We saw this one day for ourselves. Laska's wanderings brought her up against an adversary who, it turns out, was saved by a daffodil—plus that odd streak of timidity.

Peg and I were visiting some friends. They'd wanted to meet our wolfdog, so we brought her along. Her eighty pounds had been cramped in the back seat of the car for hours so, after they had seen her a few minutes, we let her explore her new surroundings.

✵ ✵ ✵

After we'd gone indoors, Spike Speidel glanced outdoors and noticed her. "Look over toward the next house, Ron."

We went to the window. A lawn stretched between Jo and Spike's house and that of their neighbors. Scattered over the lawn were a few solitary daffodils. Standing stiffly, hair abristle, tail indecisively at half mast, and staring intently toward a daffodil six feet from her nose, was Laska.

Underneath that daffodil, also with every hair on end, was her antagonist: a half-size kitten.

As we watched, Laska slowly made a big circle around her tiny foe. The kitten turned with her. When they'd almost gone the complete circle, Laska stepped on a twig. We saw a branch rise up, then fall as it snapped.

That snap did it. The kitten spat and swiped outward with its paw. Laska did a hasty retreat—almost a somersault. Now, ten feet away, she stopped.

Apparently this was too much. The kitten all by itself was bad enough: sheltered by the daffodil it was wellnigh invulnerable.

Suddenly a clump of grass seemed to catch her interest. The grass was about twenty feet away, in the opposite direction. With a casual about-face she turned away from the kitten. Then she trotted toward the clump.

From there she investigated the driveway. Then the telephone pole. Then the rosebush, the sidewalk, and

the front door. Never once did she glance back at that offending feline, there under the daffodil.

Laska, the eighty pound Amazon, had been faced
down by a kitten.

But that was our wolfdog—a strange mixture of the
wild and the domestic, the bold and the fainthearted.
The dog reveling in the luxury of the rug and the wolf
concerned about the welfare of the pack.

I guess we most felt like members of her pack on that
sleepy Sunday morning in June. I was hoping to gain
forty last winks, but Laska was wide awake. She woofed
and whined and carried on in her pen. It was the time
we usually arose and she was ready for the day.

I made my way out to her yard. Opening the door, I
let her loose. Going back to bed, I left the outside door
open. She'd return in five minutes, as soon as she'd
made the rounds of the driveway. Then, I hoped, she'd
settle down near the bed until we awakened.

I'd gone back to sleep. Slowly I became aware that
she had returned and was standing near the bed. There
was a sudden retching sound—and Laska threw up on
the rug.

I jumped up. But she wasn't sick. Not at all. Indeed,
she sat back, ears pricked up and tail wagging. Plainly—
or so it seemed to me—the wolf in her had played out a
little drama.

Wolves cannot travel in packs all the time, of course.
When a mother has pups or when some member is ill,
there's a need for food to be brought back to the den. So

the wolf has developed an efficient way to carry it—in its stomach. Then, at the den, the food is regurgitated for the waiting family.

Possibly it had been Laska's turn to do the hunting. Peg and I had remained home in the "den." And she had done her work well. For that apparent attack of indigestion was merely her unselfish contribution to the welfare of our little pack—a half-grown woodchuck.

Nor does there seem to be an end to such events. It's hard, often, to separate the wolf—if indeed, it can be done, as many traits are common to both.

Dogs and wolves both pant when they're hot. They both bury bones and similar leftovers. They both roll in dead squirrels, expired birds' eggs, and other delicacies.

One time at the Bronx Zoo I watched a pair of timber wolves behaving just like their domestic counterparts. A bird of some sort had expired in their fenced enclosure. It was hard to tell what kind of bird it was, except that it had gray feathers.

No—I'll take that back. One could easily tell what kind of bird it was: a long dead and highly aromatic one. The wolves made this fact abundantly clear. First one animal and then the other would sniff at the touseled mess with surpassing interest. Then it would rub head, neck, and shoulders, and finally its whole body in that gorgeous perfume, cavorting with legs waving in the air like any pampered pooch over some long-expired leftovers on garbage day.

Laska revels in such delights when she can, of

course. We'll not soon forget her meeting with the unfortunate toad, for instance.

The toad, done in by some malady, had found a resting place among the plants of our hillside herb garden. Laska sniffed it out and proceeded to cover every available inch of herself with as much toad scent as possible.

The end result wasn't half bad, however. Every time she'd roll in the toad it'd slip a bit further downhill. Thus she ran the gamut of the garden while pursuing that extinct but elusive amphibian. Later, when she came and joined us, the odor of toad was tempered—in fact overwhelmed—by the aroma of peppermint sauce.

Another event could have been the action of either dog or wolf. Peg and I keep a supply of birdseed and suet at our feeder. The best suet, we feel, is the fat around the kidney of beef. It's firm, almost flaky, and strongly resists melting in the afternoon sun at the back door.

We'd just obtained some of this kidney suet. I put it in the hanging feeder, tossing the old piece out to Laska. When I was through hanging up the new food, I brought our pup into the house. Then Peg and I sat down to lunch.

Laska seemed uneasy. She paced up and down. She paid little attention to our lunch, but seemed to be searching for something. After several minutes, she walked over to our big picture window. A large cactus plant was growing there in a big wooden pot.

We watched as our wolfdog set something down. It

was the suet. She'd apparently been carrying it around for about fifteen minutes. Avoiding the spines of the cactus, she carefully pushed a hole in the soil with her nose.

Without a look back to see if we approved, she solemnly buried the smelly suet in our big flowerpot.

Then, her canine duty done, she lay down and went to sleep.

Although Laska is now a firm Number Three on the totem pole, she wasn't necessarily that secure from the start. In other words, she had to find her place. She had to test my authority.

It happened one evening when she had nearly attained her full growth. Peg and I had been away for supper. Coming home, we were serenaded by a howling, woofing, whining Laska in her yard.

"Just some bones for you tonight," I told our vociferous pet. "No walk. It's time for everybody to go to sleep." And with that I tossed her the contents of a doggie bag we'd brought home from the restaurant. Laska gobbled the bones almost before we got in the house. Then she became more garrulous than ever.

She'd quiet down, I told myself. Tie, jacket, and shoes off, I flopped down in the chair. But the howls and wails came loud and clear.

Going to the back door, I flipped on the light. "No!" I told her. "No more noise tonight!"

That'd fix her. It did, too—until I'd gone inside again. Then the clamor started once more.

LASKA

"Does she have water?" Peg asked.

"Yep."

"Her foot's not caught in the wire fence or anything?"

"Nope. She started jumping the way she always does when I looked out at her."

"Well, Dearie—time for your walk, I guess."

I'd hoped to get out of my usual evening ritual of trudging down the driveway while our pup frolicked around me, but Laska would have none of it. From the sounds, she wasn't about to quit, so I tossed on an outer jacket and boots. Then I went to let out Lady Loudmouth.

I realized my mistake the minute I unlatched the door. Scuttling out between me and the doorpost, Laska raced off into the darkness. Bushes rattled, leaves rustled, twigs and branches broke as she crashed her way into the woods.

"No!" I yelled. "Laska! No!"

The crashing stopped—momentarily. I shouted again. But now that I was out of sight, I couldn't glare at her to reinforce my command. So she was off once more.

Peg had heard it all. As I burst into the door, she met me with the big flashlight. "Do you want me to go too?"

"No!" I snapped, almost as loud as I'd yelled at Laska. Peg recoiled in mock horror.

Outside again, I could hear the commotion in the woods. Now there was a snarling and chattering along with the sound of the underbrush. Laska had cornered a raccoon.

♦ ♦ ♦

Yelling all the while, I hurtled through the bushes.
Branches whipped my face. Roots reached up and
clutched at my legs. Slippery leaves and hummocks and
rocks made me flounder and fall. The more I stumbled
the madder I got.

As I rounded a hemlock tree, my flashlight caught
Laska and the raccoon. They were at the base of a big
maple. The 'coon was little more than half grown, weighing perhaps eight pounds. The battle was apparently a
standoff: the 'coon was well protected by the roots of
the tree.

Laska took one look at me bearing down on her. She
quit the fight and vanished into the darkness. The raccoon scampered away and up a smaller tree. I inspected
it as best I could from the ground. Then, seething more
at Laska's disobedience than at the damage she may have
done to the raccoon, I stumbled my way back to the
house.

Laska had arrived ahead of me. Peg had let her in.
Now the perfidious pup crouched beneath the table.

There. Dead to rights. I'd fix her.

I grabbed the first weapon that came to hand: a
stuffed toy on the sofa. Then I gave Laska a lesson in
obedience at the top of my voice—punctuated by blows
from the stuffed animal.

It was hard to discipline her, down there under the
table like that. In the course of one particularly emphatic
point the toy caught on the corner of the table. It flew
against the wall.

LASKA

Peg stepped over and picked it up. Then she handed it to me without a word. Laska took advantage of the occasion to scuttle away and into the room down the hall. There she managed to scramble under the bed.

For the first time I noticed the weapon I'd been using. Peg's mother had been on a visit to our house and, as luck would have it, she'd forgotten a favorite sofa pillow she carried with her. It was a smiling, portly raccoon—and weighing perhaps eight ounces.

I looked at Laska, down in that room. All I could see was a pair of blue eyes, unblinking in the gloom beneath the bed. Then I glanced at my wife.

"A toy raccoon!" she gasped, collapsing on the sofa, "you beat up a wolf—with a toy raccoon!"

CHAPTER

XI

AFTER SOMEONE HAS MET OUR WOLFDOG the question arises"—but can she do any tricks?"

She most certainly can. However, we haven't taught them to her. Most of them she has learned herself. She'll "come" and "stay" on command. These she has known from her early puppy days. We also worked with her until she'd walk quietly on a leash with us. And notice that word "quietly": this is a big help, considering the size and strength of a creature that could pull us right off our feet.

I suppose we could also have taught her to roll over or stand on her hind legs. However, we were more interested in the part of her that is timber wolf. So, most of the time, we let her act naturally. In this way we hope to learn as much about the wolf in her as possible.

As with all dogs, she needs her exercise. Since she is also a sled dog, we had a harness made for her. That eighty pounds of muscle, pulling with all four feet, can move most adults on hard-packed snow. She can also pull our grandchildren, Josh, Jake, Jenny, Jared, and Amber. All together they weigh about a hundred and fifty pounds.

Here is where one of her self-taught "tricks" comes in. If the load is too big she suddenly becomes "lame." Limping on one foot, she drags the sled as if in terrible pain. The first time she did this I stopped the sled quickly to find the trouble. She held her right front foot up as if she'd stepped on something sharp. We could find nothing the matter, but unhitched her anyway.

Her trouble stopped at once. We decided she had just been fooling, so we put her back in harness. And there was the limp again—but this time in the left foot.

She has also learned how to disobey a command while obeying it—strange as that may sound. When I call her to come to me, for instance, she runs in my direction. Then, just as she gets near me, she puts on added speed. Her ears prick up and she shows a sudden interest in something just beyond me. She speeds right past me if I'm not quick to stop her. But often her act is so good that I let her go, just to see what's so important off there to the side.

Actually it is a sort of game. If I don't stop her, she may dash another hundred feet at top speed. Then she loses steam. She seems to lose interest in the strange object, too—an object that probably was not there in the first place. And back she comes.

People have studied wolves for years, even if only to learn how to destroy them. Hunters, trappers, ranchers who raised sheep and cattle have planned and calculated how to outsmart the wolf. And almost always, in their yarns, their campfire songs, the folk tales handed from one to another—and the accounts of the preceding night's forays recited through gritted teeth—they have told of the great creature's cleverness and intelligence.

It's no coincidence that renegade animals in the final days of the war on wolves were known as Old Three Toes, or One Eye, or Peg Leg. Each had had a narrow brush with a trap or gun or poison. Each had learned its lesson well. It would not be caught again until old age, exhaustion, or the overwhelming force of men and dogs drove it to its last stand.

We could see this ancient ancestry in our wolf dog. She had an impressive ability to size up a situation. More than once, in fact, she has foiled our own plans by some action of her own. In other words she has outmaneuvered us.

For example, take that common training method of giving a pet a reward for good behavior. When the animal does the trick or follows the command, there's a pleasant result: it gets a tidbit, perhaps, or warm praise and a pat on the head. Laska, quite naturally, seemed to enjoy such sessions. Small-sized Milk Bone biscuits were especially prized, and we saved them just for these occasions. Good behavior or obedience to a command meant a tasty biscuit. Lackluster actions, or slowness to obey, no reward.

Hence the Case of the Bedtime Snack.

LASKA

On nights when she was to stay in the house, we'd let our wolfdog out for a few minutes just before retiring. After she had relieved herself out under the pines somewhere, she'd come prancing back to the door. We'd give her a Milk Bone for such a prompt and forthright performance—and she'd settle down for the rest of the night.

Then came one of the coldest Januarys on record. The temperature never got above zero Fahrenheit, even in the daytime, for more than two weeks. When we walked through the wintry landscape, we could feel tiny frost slivers as our breath crystallized momentarily on our lips. When we blinked, our eyelashes often froze together.

Although Laska's doghouse was snug and she was used to the cold weather, we decided that nights at thirty below zero might be a little chilly. So we placed a rug for her in the house.

We'd let her out just before bedtime. She'd disappear momentarily; then back she'd come, tail wagging, looking for that snack. "Sure got her trained," I exulted to Peg after about a week of her little evening trips out under the snowy pines. "Only took ten seconds tonight."

"Ten seconds? She could hardly make it out and back in ten seconds, Ron. To say nothing of any bathroom duties."

"But I timed her, Peg. Everything in ten seconds."

"Not *everything*, Sweetie."

So to prove her wrong I took the flashlight out into the snow. There were Laska's tracks all right—out beyond the circle of illumination of the back door light. I followed them under the big red pine. They made a little foray into the unbroken snow. When out of sight, she'd paused—unproductively—for what might be termed the proper amount of time. Then she'd returned triumphantly to the house.

Our wolfdog had gone out into the wintry night on command. She'd disappeared for awhile and then come back. So she had gone through all the steps and—sure enough—gained her reward.

Well, not all the steps. And we'd not have discovered the omission if she'd been able to judge the time. Somehow our insistence that she go out for toilet duties whether she needed them or not reminded me of a definition I once heard of a certain article of clothing: "A sweater," the definition said, "is something a youngster wears when Mother feels cold."

Apparently, Laska didn't need those nightly forays anyway. She seemed no more eager to go out in the morning after we stopped letting her out before bedtime. Her capacity to retain was simply a lot greater than we had estimated.

Another bit of deception came after I'd shut her in her enclosure. I went around to the front yard and began to prune some bushes. She could hear me working, no doubt, but could not see me. She whined and yipped and yelped as if that drafty pen was giving her pneumonia, but I kept on working. After awhile the pitiful pleading stopped. Good, I told myself, she's finally given up.

Suddenly there was an uproar behind the house: growls and snarls and deep-throated barks. Alarmed, I rushed around the corner to see what was the matter.

There was our courageous canine, hair abristle, staring down the driveway. It looked as if we were about to be attacked—but by what I did not know.

And neither did Laska. The minute she saw me the growling stopped. Whirling, she jumped and leaped at the gate, white paws beating on the wood. Obviously the invisible intruder had never existed. To turn the old fable around, she was the wolf who'd cried "boy!"

One of the outstanding gifts of the wolf is a long memory. "Once bitten, twice warned," kept many a wolf from that second mistake with trap or pitfall or glint of rifle barrel in the forest. Laska had a brush with a porcupine when she was still little more than a puppy; she has never gone near another.

The prickly creature was apparently nosing around at the edge of the woods. Our pup brought back half a muzzle full of those white quills with their pointed black tips. We took her to a veterinarian who gave her a knockout shot and pulled out the spines. Since then, porcupines have waddled across the field at the edge of the forest, and even investigated the edibility of the cedar boards at the corner of our garage, but Laska has learned her lesson. She will have nothing to do with them. Even when some amorous porky goes wailing through the woods on an autumn evening, squalling at the top of his voice, she scarcely pricks an ear. The porcupine, her attitude says, is not my cup of tea. Not any more.

One Friday afternoon we were going away for a couple of days. Peg had made a batch of applesauce; I took the apple cores and peelings out past our wolfdog's yard and down the path to the compost heap. Tossing Laska a bone on the way back, I packed the last of the things into the car and we headed off for a long weekend. A friend would care for Laska, although he wasn't to let her out of her enclosure. We didn't want her to get into trouble while we were away.

We got back after dark on Sunday evening. I could hear our pet jumping and yowling a greeting there in her yard. After we had brought in a few things from the car, I opened the gate. Instead of running from one of us to the other as she usually did, she made one bound out of the yard, spun in a right angle turn, and raced down toward the compost pit.

It had been two full days since I'd dumped those apple peelings. Laska was back in a minute; apples are not on her menu. But for more than forty-eight hours she'd been curious as to what had been tossed there.

We were able to put that impressive memory to use in keeping her away from the road, as well. Our property is shaped like the capital letter "L." The base of the "L" runs along the New Haven River for nearly a quarter mile while the upright stem pokes up beyond our house and into the woods. The road lies beyond the river, with a wooden bridge connecting it to our property, near the corner of the "L." Therefore, we figured, to keep Laska from walking out into the road all we had to do was teach her not to cross the bridge.

If she could remember a porcupine so well, and keep my visit to the compost pile in mind all weekend, maybe she could be taught the bridge was off limits. The problem was to impress her enough. Other dogs traveled that road. An occasional jogger jogged past. All of these could tempt an active pooch. What she needed, we figured, was something that would speak plainer to her than a stern "no!" even when we weren't around.

It was a matter of life or death, perhaps—her life or death. We had to have something that would be unforgettable. Even if a jogger, a kid on a bike, and a couple of dogs all trouped past at once. So we decided on the shock treatment. Literally.

It came about as we contemplated the possibility of putting some sort of gate across the bridge to keep her in her place. "What about an electric fence?" Peg asked.

"Sure—and how would cars get in and out without stopping to disconnect it?"

"Well—Laska goes barefoot, doesn't she?"

I didn't understand. But Peg pointed out the steel ramp that led from the gravel driveway up onto the wooden surface of the bridge. "If that steel plate was electrified and Laska stepped on it . . ." she said.

"Good heavens, Peg! She'd get fried!"

"No more than cows and horses do when you fence in the pasture."

"But a big horse weighs half a ton. Laska's only about the size of a fourth-grade kid. That's a lot of zap for seventy-eighty pounds."

"Maybe. But you and I have both touched that fence more than once. And we're still here."

She was right. An electric fence, while unpleasant, has more surprise than substance. Its shock is something like the spark you get when you rub your feet on a rug and touch a metal doorknob. Only more so, of course. Perhaps it was worth a trial, at that.

So we lifted up the free edge of the metal ramp and put dry pieces of wood beneath it so it'd not be grounded. Then I hid our electric fence charger in the grass nearby and connected it to the steel.

We gingerly tried it out by touching the metal with a blade of grass. The grass, being a poor conductor, allows just a bit of the current through, so you get a faint buzz if the charger is working.

It buzzed. Now for Laska's lesson.

We released our unsuspecting Laska. Then we strolled down the driveway toward her booby trap.

She frolicked ahead and around us. Casually walking closer, we headed for the bridge. We decided we'd let her discover it by herself. To call attention to it in some way might serve to implicate us in the plot. We wanted it to be a matter between her and the bridge.

She ran to the bridge. Then she disappeared beneath it. She reappeared on the other side, poking through the chokecherry bushes that grew near the river. Back up she came with the remains of a long-dead fish. She solemnly placed it on the lawn and proceeded to roll in it in an apparent transport of ecstasy.

Peg managed to get her attention long enough so I could filch the fish and hastily toss it away. Then we continued our walk. Back and forth, back and forth we went on the driveway, while that uncooperative pup went everywhere but where she should. She sampled a chipmunk hole, bounded after a robin on the lawn, sat down and scratched her ear. Then, in case you've wondered if dogs ever find the bones they've buried, I've got the answer: they do. Or at least Laska did. She dug under a lilac bush, exhumed the well-seasoned remains of a beef rib, and trotted off to deposit her prize elsewhere.

At this rate she'd never get her education. She might have meandered another half hour if Duffy hadn't come to the rescue.

Janice had let him out her front door earlier, there in her yard by the end of the bridge. The little black fellow had been lying on the lawn, watching our unusual performance. Now he got up to join the promenade.

And *he* knew what to do. Without hesitation or rehearsal. Trotting straight along the driveway, fluffy tail

※ ※ ※

wagging on high, he sauntered right onto that platform.

It jumped up and bit him. Or so it must have seemed. He gave a startled yelp and leaped backward. But he was still partly across that fateful apron. This time the shock must have been stronger in his rear portion. The poor pup scuttled frantically out onto the planks as if he'd been hit from behind by a broom.

He ran halfway across the bridge, yelping with every leap. Then he sat down and looked back at the offending apron, still yipping.

None of this was lost on Laska. At the first sound from Duffy she headed toward him. When he put it in high gear, she broke into a trot. By the time he'd escaped to the middle of the bridge, she was on the hot spot herself. Three feet landed on the metal as a hind foot was still on the driveway.

With an agonized yowl she jackknifed ahead. Three leaps brought her alongside the suffering Duffy. Three more and she was nearly at the other end of the bridge. Then she stopped. Together they sat and looked at us and whined.

We were impressed. It had worked. Too well, in fact. Both dogs were out on the bridge—on the wrong side of the fence, so to speak. How would we get them back?

It wouldn't do any good to shut off the current and lead them back; this'd cancel out what they'd learned. Besides, from their pitiful appearance, they'd have to be dragged anyway.

So I went up and got the car. Driving across the now

switched-off ramp, I picked up the two confused ca-
nines. A short ride down the road and back, and they
were returned to the right side of the bridge.

When I let them out, they frolicked as if the whole affair had never happened. What had they learned? Anything? Nothing?

Our mail carrier helped supply the answer. We were
standing by the edge of the bridge talking with Janice
when Bill McKean clattered up in his jaunty little
Bronco. When he'd deposited the mail in the boxes out
by the road I started across the bridge. Laska and Duffy
started, too—but stopped short. Duffy sat and watched
while his large companion walked warily back and forth.
She carefully sniffed the ramp; then sat down with
Duffy. They were obediently waiting when I returned
with the mail.

Success. And the lesson stayed. At least with Laska.
Duffy, living and playing right by the edge of the bridge
every day, had a difficult time discovering where driveway ended and bridge began in those months when the
snow was piled deep. After a good winter the mailbox at
the far end of that bridge was once again part of his daily
rounds.

Laska never really got over that single jolt. Once or
twice—for instance, when a neighbor rode by on her
horse, accompanied by a couple of dogs—our companionable canine found the temptation too much. However, even today, seven years after that memorable

morning in May, she merely goes to the bridge, takes a casual glance across, and turns away.

She doesn't cross the bridge. But now and again there may be something particularly attractive on the other side. She stands there with those black-rimmed ears pricked up and that tail faintly wagging. Then I recall the words of my friend, Elsie Matson, who trains and raises dogs: "Where a dog is looking, there a dog is thinking."

So I reinforce that long-ago lesson with a sharp "no!" Laska looks at me; the ears relax, the tail subsides—and the bridge is off limits again.

The taboo against crossing the bridge was mainly so our wolfdog would not be hit by a car. That road is paved and smooth and straight—a perfect invitation to a young person wishing to see how many seconds it takes to get a car to sixty miles an hour from a standing start. Indeed, we discovered, we live alongside "Rood's Run," as it's known to my youthful hightailing friends.

Actually, I'm not greatly perturbed by the occasional squeal of tires and roar of motor. I'd rather see a kid thrash the last ounce of effort out of a car then return to an earlier day when you proved yourself by how fast your horse would go. Yet I'm still glad Laska has not forgotten her little training session. And never was I more grateful than on that October morning.

I had just finished a number of letters in anticipation of the mailman's daily visit. Tossing on a light jacket, I opened the gate to Laska's yard. With her romping ahead of me, I headed down the driveway toward the bridge and the mailbox.

As usual, she was waiting for me at the bottom of the driveway. Commanding her to stay in place, I went across the bridge with the mail.

After depositing the letters I stood there a moment, taking in the scene around me. The flaming reds and yellows of the sugar maples contrasted with the dark green of spruces and firs on the hillside. A catbird called from along the river, apparently in a farewell to these hills for another year. Crickets and grasshoppers warming in the sun after the cool night tuned up their chorus.

It was a delightful morning, alive with the sounds and scents and sights of autumn. Everything seemed so easygoing and peaceful.

No. Not everything. As I started back across the bridge my gaze fell on an object in the dust by the edge of the road. Half the size of a lemon, partly covered with sand where it had rolled along the roadside, it was a tightly-pressed ball of hamburger.

What was a chunk of ground beef doing there by our mailbox? Who would lose a handful of meat like that? As I contemplated that bit of hamburger, another question formed itself in my mind. Why was it shaped so carefully, anyway? Was something hidden inside it?

I found a piece of bark from a dead tree by the bridge. Carefully scooping the meat onto the bark, I looked for other chunks. There were three more just like it.

Piling them on the bark, I took them back to where Laska waited. "Oh, no, you don't," I told her as she sniffed at what I was carrying. "You don't even get close. Something tells me this isn't good for you."

Carefully juggling my unusual find, I took it back up the driveway. Then, on the workbench in the garage, I dissected those chunks of meat.

There were two small pills in each.

Tranquilizers? I doubted it. Not vitamin pills, either. More like poison.

I had no way of knowing what those pills contained. But they'd been put in the ground beef and dropped there on purpose—and for whom?

Probably not for Jan and Steve's dog. Vocal but friendly, Duffy seemed to be almost universally liked by all who came to visit. Scarcely bigger than a tomcat, he represented little threat to anything larger than a rabbit. No—it couldn't be Duffy.

And so it had to be Laska. But why? She didn't bark. She never strayed beyond earshot, even on those occasions when I let her out and forgot her. Nor, since that fracas with the raccoon, had she even entered the woods. So I was sure she couldn't have run afoul of some hunter or, worse, gone off on the trail of a deer.

No, it was nothing she had done. But then, as I pondered, John Trotier's words came back to me—how

139

LASKA

Laska's mother had been killed, not for *who* she was, but *what* she was: an animal who bore the blood of wolves in her veins.

And here it was again. Right at the end of our bridge—the unreasoning, unjustified, senseless fear and hatred of the wolf.

Well. The fewer people who knew about this, the better. Perhaps, if nothing was said, someone would tip the scales with a chance remark that'd help me solve the mystery. I carefully dried the pills for a couple of days. Then I placed them in a little vial marked "Poison."

They are there today. Laska was unharmed. And, now that it is half a dozen years later, the person who dropped those chunks of meat should have had plenty of time to reconsider. Apparently so; as far as I know, Laska's life has not been threatened again.

One bit of good came out of that narrow escape. We made certain more than ever that our wolfdog stayed away from Rood's Run. Every chance I get, I stress that her territory ends where that bridge begins.

While the bridge is off limits, the river is not. Or so we discovered one day when we went to visit our friends at their vacation retreat.

Bob and Betty Douglas have built a small A-frame summer cottage about an eighth of a mile down the road from our bridge. It's across the valley from our property and at the end of the woods. One Saturday Bob and

Betty were there, cooking hamburgers, tossing horse-
shoes, and generally enjoying a late afternoon with some
friends who'd accompanied them.

We'd been invited, too. I let Laska have a brief run
before putting her back in her yard with her supper. But
when I called five minutes later, she didn't come running.

After a few more minutes we gave up. It wasn't like
her not to come right back after that brief inspection of
the driveway, but we decided not to wait any longer.
The hamburgers were sizzling, we knew, at the A-frame.
So we walked down the driveway, across the bridge, and
down the road to our friend's picnic.

And—you guessed it. There was Laska. Soaking wet
and welcoming us to the picnic. Apparently a playful
breeze had carried the sound of laughter and horse-
shoes. The smell of hamburgers, too. It had proved too
much for her and she had trotted along the edge of the
river until she was opposite the cottage. Then she'd
plunged in and joined the party.

Generally the ability to rise to meet the occasion is
considered desirable in a pet. And, of course, there's no
real way to tell how much of this capacity comes from the
wolf in Laska and how much from the dog in her.

In the background, there is the wolf. Always the
wolf. Where other dogs might be lying in that commodious yard and basking in the sun, Laska would walk up

and down like the caged animal she is. Often the pacing was done to the accompaniment of a woof and a bark and a whine. Sometimes it was done without a sound.

It was the silence that bothered me most. I never knew how many times she coursed back and forth behind that wire. In my mind's eye I could see her, perhaps in the middle of the night or in the heat of the day when we were not there, trotting to one corner of the yard and then another. There she'd pause and quietly look up toward the woods or beyond the fields or over the mountains.

There was something else done without a murmur. At least we never heard it. This was a quiet and determined attack on the gate.

The gate to her yard is a wooden framework with the bottom half covered with heavy wire. One day I noticed a few chips on the ground. I figured they were the aftermath of one of her favorite pastimes—chewing on any old chunk of wood that might take her fancy. But the next day there were more chips. And more the day after that.

Looking around I discovered the source of the chips: the upper portion of the gate, near where it was hooked. She had to stand on her hind legs to reach that high, so we figured it was no idle play. She'd seen me unlock the hook up there and was apparently trying to get at it the only way she could: from the inside.

As I considered that restless creature, I winced inwardly as I thought of my own rule against trying to make a pet of a wild animal. Here was one, right in her yard and in our yard. When she looked at me I sometimes felt it was almost an accusation. All her training, her quickness to learn somehow did not matter much. Not around our house and home, at least.

What mattered was the wolf. The hidden, unyielding wolf that would be forever captive.

CHAPTER

XII

I T MUST HAVE BEEN an experience to live back in the days when there really were wolves in the woods. To see the mark of a giant footpad in the damp earth, to hear a distant howl in the dark and perhaps to see a shadow moving through the trees—these must have made the hair creep on many a person's spine. And to hear the howls of a great wild symphony off in the forest doubtless caused parents to gather their children close and double check the locks on house and barn and stable.

Small wonder there were countless wolf stories. Although now, some centuries later, there's no authentic case of a single unprovoked wolf attack on a human being, those early settlers had no such reassurance. Diaries, journals, logbooks from more than a century ago tell of all manner of encounters and supposedly narrow escapes.

Many of the stories seem to be variations on a common theme: somebody's going along the road and is set on by a pack of wolves. The relentless creatures follow close at the heels of the frightened person, who usually is on horseback or riding in a wagon. They are foiled as the fugitive tosses one item after another in their path.

In Montpelier, Vermont, for instance, a man named Clark barely escaped with his life and that of his team as he was returning from a visit to town. He'd not have lived to tell the story if he hadn't had just the items to hinder the ravenous creatures: the week's supply of groceries, tossed out one by one.

Here in the town of Lincoln, the man's name was Goodrich. His tickets to life were sacks of grist from the local grain mill. Getting rid of them slowed his pursuers down, lightened the load for his horses, and got him to safety in the nick of time.

A woman in Connecticut two centuries ago was less fortified. All she had was herself and her horse. Plus a jacket. So she flailed at the wolves with the jacket until they tore it to shreds. The shirtwaist went next. Then a few layers of skirts and petticoats. Luckily she arrived at a homestead before the Moment of Truth, so to speak. The wolves followed her right to the door—whether from hunger or curiosity is not recorded.

There's a shred of truth in all these accounts. That truth is not hard to discover, either, if you consider the nature of the wolf. It is a predator, and a large one. Every potential source of food must be investigated. For creatures able to bring down a moose or elk, a horse could have seemed an intriguing quarry. Especially when it ran at their approach.

The presence of a human being along with the horse must have been of little account of those wolves of long ago. They hadn't yet learned to shy away from contact with humans. And even if they had, their curious scrutiny on the road behind the horse or wagon would probably have been enough to start a headlong flight to safety. Whether the wolves actually followed or not, they *could* have. And thereby hangs the tale.

Not always was there a horse, however. One account tells of a schoolboy who narrowly escaped a pack of wolves as he was walking home. His weapon was a stick.

His tale of the encounter aroused the little town. The next morning a posse of half a thousand men and boys headed for where the wolves were hiding. They rounded the beasts up and dispatched all seven of them.

This, too, may bear a germ of truth. That happened in 1803 and the town was Berlin, Vermont—little more than a backwoods community carved from the wilderness. Those opportunistic wolves could well have walked out and sized up a small boy all by himself on a country road. As for the battle with the stick—well, no good tale should lose in the telling.

You can find similar accounts in the history and folklore of many towns around the globe. Wolves have long made their homes in Northern Europe, Asia, and North America. On our continent, variously known as gray or

♉ ♉ ♉

timber wolves, they have ranged down into Mexico. Their roving packs knew no state or national lines. Wherever there was suitable prey, the predators would follow. The Lewis and Clark journal tells of the great herds of buffalo "attended by their little shepherds, the wolves."

With the clearing of the land and the spread of civilization across our country, ranchers and farmers appeared with their poultry and livestock. In place of alert, fleeting deer or belligerent moose, the wolves found clumsy sheep, tasty lambs, fat hogs, and calves that could easily be cut out from a herd of cattle by a few clever maneuvers.

It took little activity by the wolves to secure the attention of those early settlers. Although humans were the intruders, it was the wolf that must go. And the hunt was on.

The wolf's natural cleverness might still have saved the day. It could learn to avoid the trap, stay clear of ambush, let a poisoned carcass strictly alone. But at least two factors worked to bring about its downfall.

The first factor is the intense and unswerving loyalty of the wolf. Not only is there the constancy of one mate toward another, but there is a strong bond between members of the pack. After all, they are often of the same family. They have run together, eaten together, faced storms and privation together for as many as six or seven years.

This loyalty will lead one wolf to help a wounded companion. It may bring food to another in a trap. It may even soak its fur in a nearby stream and lie near the captive. Thus the thirsty one can chew on the fur and get a bit of moisture.

Hunters were quick to turn this closeness against the wolves. A trapped animal would be left there in hopes others would approach and be trapped or shot themselves. Wolf puppies were dug from their dens and tethered so their cries would bring the parents. A dead wolf would be dragged along by a rope so others would follow the trail to their doom.

Even such tactics would not forever fool the discerning, intelligent creature. Indeed, the specter of the lone wolf often arose because of one or two family members who learned to escape the fate of their relatives. But a second and more serious threat awaited the animal: its need for a large amount of space.

The wolf cannot change its hunting methods. A pack may travel twenty miles a night, twenty the next, and so on; thus its territory may cover a tremendous area. Such an active life is necessary if the members are to find the large amount of food needed for themselves and the families back home.

When there were large tracts of wilderness, the free-running wolves met with few serious obstacles. But as that wilderness became cut up, first by a settler's cabin here and there, and then by villages and towns, the wolves had to move on. They sought other wild areas—

and there, too, they were ousted. So their domain steadily shrank.

Even in large forested zones where the woods might make up three quarters of the total area—as is the case with my state of Vermont, for instance—the wolf today would find it impossible to make a living. Those forests are cut up by a superhighway here, a village there, a camping area over there. The great blocks of solitude are gone forever.

Thus the loss of living space speeded up the demise of the wolf. As civilization flooded forward, the wolf retreated. Now it exists only in a few pockets in our contiguous forty-eight states, mostly in wild portions of Minnesota, Michigan's Isle Royale National Park and one or two other possible haunts. Canada and Alaska have a small population. The related red wolf is making its last stand, as well, in Louisiana, Arkansas, eastern Texas, and Oklahoma.

The passing of the wolf was virtually complete in our northeast by the turn of the century. The last recorded Vermont animal was done in by a posse of farmers and townspeople on Aldis Hill in St. Albans in 1902. Peg and I visited the site some seventy years later. There's a monument commemorating the event where, according to a local account, "Mr. Brainerd fired, and the great beast made one plunge forward, struck his head to the ground, turned a complete somersault, and lay dead with a bullet in his heart."

The wolf is gone, but, as with nearly everything in

nature, it had its place. Along with that other large predator, the mountain lion, the wolf had been a part of the natural food chain. Together they lived in harmony with an incredible abundance of wildlife for centuries— before we came along to save that wildlife from its enemies.

The mountain lion—or catamount or panther— scarcely exists now except in the mountainous west. There are also a few backwoods survivors in the south. So where there once were two great wild carnivores, now there are none.

Well, almost none. A need seldom exists in nature without being filled in some way. There's a good indication that the loss of our large predators is being partially met by a new wolflike creature. It trots through the woods and brushland somewhat like its large vanishing cousin, but with a few important differences.

In the first place this "new wild canid," as it is called, is smaller—perhaps 35 to 50 pounds for males; 30 for females. Thus it needs less food and can exist on a reduced range. Then, too, it seldom travels in large packs. A family may stay together for a season, but soon the youngsters go out to seek their fortunes elsewhere. If they are slow to leave, the female evicts them when the January breeding season arrives.

Sometimes known as the eastern coyote, the new wild canid has a wider food preference than the wolf. It is scarcely choosy at all. It can exist on mice, rabbits, wild grapes and other fruit, and a few hapless ground-nesting birds. It also will eat deer when it can, but a pair of eastern coyotes—even with the inept assistance of half-grown puppies—can scarcely be considered a match for a full-grown deer. Most studies show that the deer taken are either dead or previously wounded—a service for which the canid can scarcely be faulted.

One Vermonter noticed an eastern coyote in his pasture. It was acting in a most peculiar manner: running wildly to and fro, leaping and jumping and chomping its jaws. The man shot the animal and, fearing rabies, gingerly presented it to the Vermont Fish and Game Department for study.

The animal wasn't rabid at all. Its stomach was packed with grasshoppers—the very ones that had been eating the farmer's crops. Its odd behavior was because it had been snatching them out of the air. Thus, the coyote had actually been doing him a service.

Western coyotes render the same assistance to farmers and ranchers of the plains. In many areas where the coyote was once hunted to the point of extinction a penitent populace has done an about-face. Now the animal is protected for its service in ridding the land of destructive insects and rodents. Coyotes have even been imported from other areas and released so they could speedily get back to what they'd been doing in the first place.

Peg and I saw an example of the new attitude toward

the coyote when we were motoring through Kansas re-
cently. A farmer was cutting some hay in a large field.
Around he went with tractor and mower, traveling
around the perimeter of the field and gradually working
his way to the center. And diametrically opposite him,
traveling at the same speed on the other side of the field,
was a coyote.

The coyote trotted along, snooping here and there
and occasionally pouncing on something in the new-
mown hay. When the farmer got near the road we got
out to take some pictures. Seeing us, he stopped his tractor.

"Want me to smile?" he asked, following up his question with a thirty-two tooth grin.

It was my turn to smile. "Sure," I said. "And get your
friend"—I indicated the distant coyote—"to smile, too."

The farmer chuckled. "Oh *him*. I call him Harry.
Harry the Helper. He's with me every day. Never gets
closer than he is right now, but I wouldn't hurt him for
the world. Every time he jumps he's after a mouse."

We gazed at Harry, who sat down and waited for the
mowing to continue. "One time people would say I was
crazy to let a coyote wander like that," the farmer continued. "But I see those mice scoot out from in front of
the tractor wheel. 'Run while you can,' I tell the mouse.
'Harry's out to get you.' "

We took a couple of pictures, then thanked our
friend. His tractor sputtered to life and he drove on.

Harry started up, as well, and the two of them continued their strange partnership in the hayfield.

What a difference, I told myself, between this farmer and his counterpart in Texas, where I had also taken pictures a few years previously. The Texas rancher had shot or captured half a dozen coyotes. They were proudly displayed, hanging upside down, on a roadside fence.

The eastern coyote is apparently a variety of that slightly smaller western animal. Perhaps there's also a little wolf blood somewhere in its ancestry. It has most likely come from the midwest, appearing in the northeast around the 1940s. The first report of one in my Green Mountain State of Vermont was in 1948. I've seen two of the creatures in the wild—graceful runners, holding their tails low in coyote fashion, rather than above their backs as with Laska and her wolf ancestors.

I've held an eastern coyote in my arms as well—a dead female weighing twenty-seven pounds. Shot by a deer hunter ("she was after the same deer that I was") she was displayed on his porch, photographed for the local paper, and finally relegated to the town dump.

Joan Luckey, a friend of ours, is a specialist on this new arrival to the wildlife scene. Peg and I stood and chatted with her after a talk in Boxford, Massachusetts. She, too, held an eastern coyote in her arms: an alert, tawny gray female whose golden brown eyes took in every detail of her surroundings. "Pheasant," Joan told me, indicating her vibrant armful, "can help people understand more about coyotes in five minutes than a full-length movie."

Then she smiled. "—with a book tossed in for good measure."

I could readily agree. Peg and I had watched in fascination as slender, auburn-haired Joan put her unusual companion through her paces. Pheasant walked across the floor gracefully, but with a vigilance that missed nothing. A newspaper reporter turned another page of the notebook: Pheasant's gaze immediately swept in that direction. A bird flew past the window; those hazel eyes flicked to watch it. I dropped a pencil and was instantly the object of a look so piercing that I felt like apologizing.

Nor were the little actions of the hundred or so spectators lost on this finely tuned creature. Each motion, every creak of the folding chairs received momentary notice. The sudden buzz of a fly near an overhead light made her start as at the crack of a gun.

At the end of the program, as Pheasant stood on the table to be petted, it was clear that she keenly felt every hand—perhaps every finger—that touched her. Those pointed ears moved constantly as voices assailed her from all sides.

It was the first experience most of the women of that club had had with a live, uncaged predator. Joan has not tried to make a pet of this or her four other eastern coyotes, hence much of that wildness is still present.

⚜ ⚜ ⚜

"I confess I didn't feel toward Pheasant as I might feel toward a collie or a springer spaniel," one woman told me. "That almost white fur on the underside, the dark gray line along the back, the bushy tail—this is no dog."

"But," she continued, "she's not supposed to be a dog. She's a wild animal. You're interested the moment you see her. And you respect her—tremendously. Which is a new way for me to feel about beasts of prey, believe me."

I guess she said it, right there. With an experience like this a person does, indeed, look at a creature in a new way. I've found this to be the case almost without fail as I've taken one or another of our misunderstood animals with me on talks throughout our land. When you meet a creature personally, you gain a new insight into what it is really like.

Once, or instance, I presented an amicable boa constrictor to a group of schoolchildren. After they'd all handled Julius Squeezer and made his acquaintance, I asked them what they thought about snakes.

One lad voiced the feelings of many. "We cannot really tell you about snakes, Mr. Rood. Julius sort of isn't a snake. He's—well, he's Julius!"

That's the way it was with Lady the tarantula, Oscar the skunk, and Piney the porcupine. Those who got the chance to meet them lost much of their fear and distrust.

155

And an entire class cheered when Polly the garter snake nonchalantly presented us with a brand new four-inch snakelet.

Yes, Pheasant was making friends and correcting a few mistaken impressions for herself and for Joan Luckey wherever they went. The same can be said of a whole succession of the coyote's large cousins—geniune timber wolves, along with their friend John Harris.

John knows his wolves; he's had several dozen of them. Many have lived with him and his wife in a San Francisco auto junkyard. His interest in them began in the early 1960s. His wife had brought home an abandoned wolf pup from the zoo. The appealing little waif captured their hearts at once.

"As things have a way of doing," he told me, "we soon got another one. And another, and so on. The old cars made good temporary homes for them. Or at least they did until the neighbors complained."

He scratched at his thick mop of curly hair. "It got to be a problem. They were going to have the law on us. So I said, what the heck, wolves are much more interesting than junk cars, anyway. I quit the junkyard and threw my lot in with the wolves. I've been with them ever since."

John travels the entire country with two or three of his impressive wilderness companions in a special van. "And everywhere the results are the same, Ron," he told me on a recent visit to our own Green Mountain State.

"People cannot believe the warm and lively animal in front of them is the same as the cold and shadowy night creature that skulks through all those stories."

They are still wolves, he's quick to point out. "People often ask me where they can get one for a pet. I tell them there's no such thing as a pet wolf. There's just a wild animal in captivity, that's all."

His current "wild animal in captivity" is striking indeed. Slick, a tawny young male, is a cross between Alaskan and Canadian timber wolves. Born and raised in captivity, Slick is only two and a half years old as I write these words. Already, however, he weighs 140 pounds, and should add 10 or 15 pounds when he gets his full growth.

Coming into a roomful of children—or, for that matter, the Smithsonian or Carnegie Hall, where he has appeared—the great wolf silences every voice just by standing there. Together with bearded, lionesque John Harris, he is an unforgettable sight. You may see his picture for yourself on the next-to-last page of *National Geographic* for November, 1979.

John Harris and his wild canine friends have been gripping the imagination of crowds across the continent for nearly twenty years. Joan Luckey has been doing the same in the east for half that time. Both, in the opinion of many, no doubt, are waging a losing battle. But both, I believe, are doing something important. For, as I said earlier in this chapter, it must have been an experience to live back in those days when there really were wolves in the woods.

And through dedicated people like Joan and John, those days may live again, if only briefly. For a few thousand persons fortunate enough to stroke that thick fur, to contemplate those tireless legs, to gaze into the fathomless yellow brown eyes, the years may roll back indeed.

CHAPTER

XIII

AS MONTHS TURNED INTO YEARS the line between dog and wolf in Laska became more sharply drawn. Most of the time she was like lots of other dogs—companionable and easygoing. Then, as if one door had opened and another had slammed shut, she would become a wolf. Or at least a wild creature. An animal with the snap reactions of one whose existence depended on reflex and speed.

One evening, for instance, Peg and I were looking at a number of colored slides on our screen. We were going through them for a new show I was preparing. The weather outside was bitter and we had brought Laska into the house. She was asleep on the rug.

Our screen is the type that pulls down from the ceiling. After a number of slides I realized it wasn't stretched to its full length. So I went forward to pull it out some more.

Blinded by the glare of the projector, I stumbled right over the sleeping Laska. There was a snarl and a leap. Two paws slammed into my chest and I found myself looking into a mouthful of teeth. Caught off balance, I staggered backward. Laska's paws raked down my shirt as she dropped to the floor. "No!" I yelled. "No! No!"

And it was over. The teeth hadn't broken the skin but they'd actually touched me. My wolfdog retreated toward the fireplace. There, shadowy against the stark beam of the projector, she lay meekly down.

I wish such events took place when there's time to think. My clumsiness had made it happen. Now what should I do?

I should be the alpha wolf, that's what. If it had occurred out in the wild, Laska would have been put in her place.

I took her by the collar. Then I did what I'd seen one wolf do to another to settle an argument: I pinned her. Right to the floor. Pressing that muzzle to the rug, I looked into those baleful eyes from six inches away. Only the eyes weren't baleful now; they were half shut as she endured my rebuke.

"Never!" I told her. "Never again do you jump like that!"

Of course I couldn't blame her. Almost anybody with a chihuahua can tell you to let sleeping dogs lie. Yet it must not be repeated, no matter whose fault it was. Or whether it was actually a dog or a wolf that had leaped at me.

What if it had been a toddler who had made that

blunder? Laska's reaction might have frightened the youngster for life.

I held her there for a full minute. Then I released her. She lay without moving. Going back to my projector I finished the slideshow. And that's all there was to the incident.

It wasn't completely out of mind, of course. "Do you suppose she really remembers?" Peg asked one day a couple of weeks later as we were recalling the event. "Would it happen again under the same circumstances?"

"Shall I put on a parka and catcher's mask and give it a try?"

She grinned. "You could never fall all over her like that again. I'd have clobbered you myself if it'd happened to me."

We knew you cannot unlearn a reflex anyway, so we decided merely to be more careful. Since then we've accidentally bumped or touched her while she's been sleeping. The response is just as quick, but it's more suited to the occasion. We just hope a major collision won't happen a second time.

She may have better control now, at eight years of age, but we're still impressed by the speed of those reflexes. A game we used to play as kids was for one person to hold a playing card suspended lightly between the fingers. A second person, with hand held a few inches lower, would attempt to catch the card when the first person let it go. It's almost impossible even to touch

your target as it drops to the floor. No matter how hard
you concentrate, the card moves so swiftly your fingers
merely close on thin air. Your reaction is nowhere near
fast enough.

Try it yourself with a friend. You can use any other
object, provided it's thin enough or heavy enough so
wind resistance doesn't slow it down. A pebble, a
marble, even a toothpick held on end will drop to the
floor untouched.

The game is no effort at all for Laska. We use a large
dog biscuit. Positioning it so it will fall crosswise into her
mouth, we hold it at shoulder height. She sits, eyes
riveted on it at about waist level. However, she doesn't
merely catch the biscuit, she grabs it—and part of it falls
to the floor, seemingly without pausing. So sure, so pre-
cise is her chop that she catches and shatters the biscuit
all in one motion.

Barry Lopez's *Of Wolves and Men* points out the
tremendous power of those jaws as well as their swift-
ness. Careful tests have shown the strength of the wolf's
grip to measure up to 1500 pounds per square inch. This
is twice that of a wolflike dog, the German shepherd,
who can muster up a mere 750 pounds. The difference is
in bone shape and size. Plus the musculature of face and
jaw.

For all her strength and agility, there's still that
streak of timidity. As with wild wolves that have been
known to recoil from a fluttering moth, Laska may jump

❧ ❧ ❧

back from a falling leaf. A fly lands on her; its touch may seem light, but her senses are keen. Sometimes she tries to catch it but other times she may retreat, leaving the battlefield to the victorious insect.

One time we had the card table set up in the living room. Laska walked under it. On the way out her back hit the table. She yipped and scooted out of the way— ears laid back and tail tucked in. She ran across the room to where I was sitting before she looked back to see what had attacked her.

Another time I was burning some wood in the fire-place to take off the morning chill. Ordinarily we use sugar maple, which abounds in these Vermont hills and burns with a quiet, steady flame. This time, however, we were burning ends and pieces of lumber left over from the carpentry that Bob Jimmo had been doing for us. The wood was white pine, which pops and cracks and almost explodes while burning. It made an exuberant blaze. Echoing in that fireplace as in a music shell, it roared and snapped and sounded like a small war.

I poked at it and reached for more wood. As I did so, my gaze chanced to fall on our wolfdog. Somehow she'd gotten herself up on one of the tall chairs by the kitchen counter. And there she perched like an elephant on a circus stool.

"Why Laska!" I said in surprise. "We've had fires here all winter. What makes this one so different?"

In reply a pink tongue nervously circled around a

white muzzle. That bushy black tail with its white underside wagged weakly between her legs. The stool was too
small for her to sit, so she half crouched as best she
could, looking at me.

A loud snap from the fire caused her to wince. So that
was it—not the flames but the noise!

"Okay, okay," I told her. "Let's take you outside."

She leaped from the stool and bounded toward the
door. There she whirled in little circles until I let her
out.

Apparently what is fearful about fire is its unknown
quantity rather than its destructive force. A small fire
may actually draw wild animals out of curiosity. It is
usually when it becomes a roaring blaze with searing
heat that they turn and run.

To Laska all our fires had apparently been sedate af-
fairs until that startling conflagration. Nor could she
forget it; from that day every fire apparently recalled that
boisterous blaze.

She goes through quite a routine as soon as we touch
a match to the wood in the fireplace. Those ears prick
up, then lie flat against her head. That expressive tail,
which may have been lying full length on the rug, retreats so it's as close to her body as possible. She watches
the strengthening flames; then gets up and paces the
floor. She does a complete tour of the room, sneaking
behind every chair, or under every table. She finally
halts and leans right against Peg or me, whomever is
farthest from the fire.

If we're seated at the table she sneaks under it and sits on our feet. Soon a black nose appears under the table edge at somebody's place. It is followed by a whitish muzzle and a pair of pleading blue eyes. Now you have to pay attention to her. Laska, the well-behaved, the disciplined member of our little hilltop "pack," is completely flummoxed by fire. If you don't stop her, she'll try to climb up under the table edge and into your lap. All eighty pounds of her, while your supper goes sliding.

One time we had several friends as dinner guests. They wanted to meet our wolfdog so I brought her into the house. The fire was burning quietly. Under the excitement of making six new friends, she paid scant attention to it.

We sat down to our meal. Peg and I usually say grace before eating. As I spoke a few words of thanks I could feel a stealthy movement in my lap. It was just for a second; then all was serene down there. Figuring Laska had found no room under the table and had gone elsewhere, I started to serve the food.

Then Travis Harris spoke up: "Well, I'll be darned!"

He was bending down and peering under the table. We followed his example and looked too. There, draped over shoes and piled on the floor, were eight napkins. They'd been carefully removed from their respective laps and deposited there by an apprehensive Laska. Apparently all those feet and legs had been too much of a challenge. However, she'd threaded her way among them and quietly give notice of her presence anyway.

When Peg's aging mother came for a visit, we lit a fire for extra warmth. It was the first time we'd used the fireplace that autumn and we'd forgotten its effect on our wolfdog. So, bringing Laska in for company, my wife and I left the two of them together while we went to a meeting.

When we returned, Peg's mother was in the guest room with the door closed. Perhaps she'd gone to bed, we figured. However, we'd hardly taken our jackets off when the door opened. "Thank heaven you've come!" said Mother Bruce. "I was scared to death!"

"Scared? What for?"

"Your dog, Ron. Your dog attacked me."

"*Attacked* you?"

"Well, just about. I was on the sofa, watching television. Suddenly she put her paw in my lap—"

"Oh, that's her way of being friendly."

"But that wasn't all. She put the other foot up too. Then she jumped right up on me."

Of course—the fire. And our pet's private problem. "She's just afraid of fire. She was only coming to you for protection," Peg said.

At this, her mother drew herself up to her full four-feet-eleven. "And how could I protect her? I couldn't even move!"

Somehow she'd managed to escape all that unexpected togetherness. Then she had fled to the safety of her bedroom. This, of course, allowed the fire to die down. Which was good for the composure of both of them.

After we explained it all, they became friends again. But now, whenever we have occasion to leave Laska alone with people, we make sure there's no fire going. It's just one of the wild traits that came with our pet whether we wished it or not.

Another time Laska's wildness shows is when she has canine visitors. If someone brings a dog in a car, the two of them have the usual stiff-tailed sniffing and piddling match that goes on at such times. Then they begin to play.

She accepts the other dog, I assume, because it clearly arrived as a guest.

Things are about the same when the visitor arrives on foot—if it's a male. The two of them go around from tree stump to bush, solemnly "signing" each of these doggy bulletin boards. They play a little. Then Laska returns to the place she occupies by the back door when she's not shut up in her yard.

Let a female wander onto the property, however, and there's no question: this is Laska's land. Somehow, in a way I've never been able to fathom, dogs recognize each other's gender from a distance. Males are tolerated, but this female interloper must be ousted.

The visitor becomes aware of the fact, too. She may pretend a sudden interest in something behind her— and then farther behind that, and so on until she's crossed the bridge. Supervising this orderly retreat is the imperious Laska, "saying" with her eyes, her raised hackles and stiffly-erect tail that there are enough females around this pack already.

Her size, plus being on her own property, usually can provide all the authority necessary. As Robert Ardrey's *Territorial Imperative* points out, there's an enormous advantage to being on home ground. None of the wandering females has ever contested Laska's position for long, although one or two have engaged in a brief and perfunctory tussle. Then, breaking off the contest as gracefully as possible under such strained circumstances, the interloper makes her escape.

A small female beagle trotted up the driveway one morning. She had the misfortune to discover one of Laska's abandoned bones. At least the bone had given every appearance of being abandoned, lying under the pine tree like that. But the minute little Bungles—or whatever her name was—showed an interest in it, that bone became the most important item in the world.

With a snarling roar, Laska launched herself at the unfortunate beagle. There was a flurry of flying bodies. The little dog emerged at a gallop, ki-yi-yi-ing and running with all she had. Laska came close behind. The little beagle's legs pumped in desperation while her large antagonist followed in great leaps.

The unequal race disappeared down the driveway and out of sight. Then I saw the small dog fleeing up the road. Laska had chased her to the bridge. Now she returned in righteous vindication.

※ ※ ※

I considered what I had seen. That wolfdog could
have disabled the smaller animal with one chop. She
could have caught her at any point all the way down the
driveway. She hadn't. She had followed the code of
ethics practiced by the wolf and reflected in the behavior
of the dog: mercy to the vanquished.

Real fights between wolves are rare. The marvelous
chain of authority in the pack usually makes physical
combat unnecessary. And when there is a battle the one
who's losing can call off the fight. Turning belly up, ex-
posing that tender throat to those lethal jaws, the loser
says, in effect: "Here I am—defeated. I am in your
power."

Once I was the guest of Carol and Marlin Perkins at
the St. Louis Wolf Sanctuary. The Sanctuary is a fenced-
in hillside of only a few acres of bushes, open land, and a
little pond. There is an observation platform so people
can watch the wolves and take pictures.

We could see about eight animals in the enclosure.
One wolf carefully walked around a second one on its
way to a cooling dip in the pond. "They must get in each
other's way on occasion," I said.

"Well," Marlin answered, "that boss over there"—he
indicated a large male I had failed to notice before—
"doesn't tolerate any bickering. And the 'peck order'
keeps things peaceful too. Besides, if there is a spat, the
belly-up position of the loser is about like a flag of sur-
render."

His wife chuckled. "They're different from people

after an argument. Two minutes after they've settled their problem they act as if it had never happened. There's not a sign of a grudge on either side."

It was scarcely a wilderness situation, as it was only a few miles from downtown St. Louis. Then, too, there were people frequently moving about just a few feet beyond that fence. "But it's large enough so we can get a chance to look in on a pack of wolves when they're more or less at home," Marlin said.

A few days later, back in Vermont, I contemplated my own animal in her enclosure. The wolf in her paced the fence or fled from the fire or lunged, all abristle and ready for a fight, when someone accidentally tripped over her slumbering form.

Those St. Louis wolves would have done the same too—but there was a reason behind their captivity. People could study them, could learn about them. Perhaps somehow, someone could solve the problem of how to preserve such a far-ranging animal when the land available for its use is steadily shrinking.

But our wolf—what good was she? So I could show her off, like someone walking a cheetah along a city street? To trade on her reputation so people would think we had a watchdog? To say, when somebody wonders what kind of animal we have, "Oh her? She's part timber wolf"—was this the best we could do with her?

No. There had to be something more. We just had to find it, that was all.

❦ ❦ ❦

Nor would I be allowed to forget that obligation to our unusual pet. Certainly not after the day I witnessed an ancient tableau. I had read about it in books and had seen one or two pictures of it, but never expected to see it in real life.

Willie Sumner had killed one of his Angus steers and we had taken a portion of the meat. The packinghouse that had prepared it had given us a large box of bones for Laska. Included in the box were three beef ribs plus the attached vertebrae.

I gave Laska the whole chunk. She spent an hour chewing on it, pulling at muscle and gristle and cartilage. Now, satisfied, she lay near it in the afternoon sun.

Three blue jays had been sitting in a nearby tree, watching her. When she retired, they fluttered down and began to pick the bones.

It required only a bit of imagination to take that little scene back in time. Back to a forgotten period in the past, when some timber wolf, having killed the moose and eaten its fill, lay back to sleep while the waiting jays drifted down to finish off the feast.

And here it was today: the slumbering wolf, the well-gnawed portion of a skeleton and the ever-present scavenger birds. Right in my back yard.

Except there was a fence around it. And that made all the difference.

CHAPTER

XIV

A QUARTER WOLF," said David Cunningham, "is fine. Even an animal that's half wolf. There's enough domestic dog in its make-up to be trainable. It will follow orders and yield to the will of a superior human being."

He poured himself another cup of coffee. "The other portion—the half, or less, that is wolf—will have that intense loyalty and stamina and intelligence that have been in the make-up of the wolf for ages."

As he spoke, he reached down and scratched the shoulders of a large buff-colored creature who lay at his feet. "Now Tundra, here, is such an animal. In her I've got eighty-five pounds of half-and-half. But you get more wolf than dog and you've got troubles. After all, the wolf is wild. It's not meant to run meekly around the front lawn like an elderly cocker spaniel."

Dave raises hybrids between the dog and the wolf at his kennel near Vergennes, Vermont. With a foundation stock of dogs incorporating several breeds—German shepherd, for instance, Newfoundland and working collie—he has produced dozens of crosses in the last decade. It was one of such animals that had accompanied him to our meeting in a restaurant on the Vergennes Main Street. She lay quietly beneath the table—a magnificent specimen with thick fur almost the color of cream. When he petted her, she raised the brow over one golden brown eye, thumped her tail, and went back to sleep.

The restaurant was not serving regular customers. Not at the moment, anyway. It was due to open at noon. Dave and I had chosen it as a convenient spot for a morning's chat. He'd brought Tundra along in his pickup truck.

"To have a pure wolf," he continued, "you've got to be practically a lion tamer. The wolf is too independent. Collars and fences and a dish of food are not part of its life. Besides, it's one mental jump ahead of you—just about untrainable. You can't even housebreak it."

I told him of Laska's capacity for making the best of a situation; the times she had fooled us; the ways she'd coped with problems.

"And she's just part wolf," Dave reminded me. "If she was full blooded, it'd be more than you could handle. You'd end up getting rid of her. Or you'd merely have a wild animal in a cage."

With careful selection, plus complete records on the results of his breeding, Dave can control the genetic make-up of his animals. I considered the complexity of some of his crosses: three-eighths timber wolf, for instance, and five-eighths combined shepherd, Labrador, and collie. With such ancestry he can hope to get the best of several strains in one animal.

But why go to all this trouble? Ruggedly handsome as his animals are, with colors from ebony to creamy white—and many combinations of both—why raise a creature that is just a hodgepodge?

"There are several reasons," Dave said. "One is the fun and accomplishment of experimenting with a living animal. Another, I guess, is because I like large dogs the way some people like boats or horses or old coins."

He leaned back and contemplated the form of the sleeping Tundra at his feet. "But mostly, Ron, it's because I like the wolf. There's hardly a place left in Vermont where wolves could ever run free. The same could be said of almost any other state. Even you and I, who admire the wolf, make its normal life impossible merely by our presence. A human habitation, a farm dog—even a quiet little backwoods cabin—would be so upsetting to a wolf that it'd try to find another place that wasn't so crowded."

"And such a place," I added, almost unnecessarily, "hardly exists any more."

"Exactly. So that's where Tundra and Tanukie and Arctic come in. By breeding the wolf to a dog I capture the wolf. It's in my animals—diluted four to one here, and six to one there. Hidden in a way, perhaps, but it's still there in the animal's hereditary make-up."

I began to realize the implications of what he was saying. Here, at least partially, might be a way out of an almost impossible situation. The wilderness was vanishing, yes—and with it the hopes for a normal life for the wolf. But, rather than throwing up his hands and watching the wolf disappear too, Dave was at least setting aside some of that dwindling stock before it was gone. He was putting the soul in a different body, so to speak. Thus the tireless, far-running wolf would be contained within the physical body of the more easygoing dog.

"So you have a sort of gene pool there in your kennel?" I suggested. "A zoo without fences?"

"I guess you could call it that," he said. "You and I know zoos can be pretty grim places. Even the best can never approach a hundred miles of wild lands. Maybe this is another way to hold the wolf beside putting it behind bars."

We talked over another cup of coffee. And another. It has long been an intriguing thought, this crossing of two animals to gain some of the qualities of both. As kids we used to joke about the possibilities: crossing a horse with a kangaroo, for instance, so when it rained you could ride inside. Or the unlikely marriage between a parrot and a tiger. "The result didn't look like much," the joke continued,—"but when it spoke, everybody listened."

It reminded me of the suggestion supposedly made by a shapely actress to George Bernard Shaw. They should get together and produce a child, she said. Thus it would combine his brains and her body.

The playwright declined. As luck would have it, he told her, the youngster would have *her* brains and *his* body.

And what of Dave Cunningham's animals? Do they have only the good qualities of the wolf and dog? Some of the good? Some of the bad? Can you breed two half wolves together and get a whole wolf? Or—since the other half of each is dog—do you get a whole dog?

He doesn't have all the answers yet. Ten years is too short a time. "But the wolf is here," he said, thumping Tundra's shoulders as we parted at the door. "At least we've got something to work with."

As I drove home, I reflected on that final remark. He did, indeed, have "something to work with."

Perhaps it'd be impossible to get a full-blooded wolf from two half-breeds. At least with present knowledge. But that gene pool would still be there. It might be tapped more effectively years from now, from the great-great-grandchildren of Tundra or Willow, or one of Dave's other charges. Perhaps, even, some solution to the problem of shrinking wilderness would have been found. Then the wolf could return to its natural surroundings.

It was an exciting thought. Sort of like the long-considered possibility of putting critically ill human beings in a suspended, frozen state. They could be revived in the future so they could be cured by techniques unknown today.

Then came another idea. Here, at last, could be the justification for animals like Laska. The wolf in such creatures would be forever captive, true. But it would also be forever safe. And if it was passed down to future offspring, it'd be safe there as well.

Such were my thoughts as I shut off the engine and headed for the back door. Our wolfdog roused from her noonday snooze. She jumped at the gate; I let her out of the yard. Then I went in and unloaded my thoughts to my wife. "So an animal like Laska may not be wasted, Peg," I said. "It could be a sort of walking blood bank or something. Not so much a wild animal captured as a threatened animal saved."

At this point Laska came back from her run. Peg let her in, bent down and tousled her ears. "Do you feel threatened, Laska?" she asked.

Then she straightened up. "It may be fine for Dave to have a dozen little wolf pups running around his property," she said, "but Laska's been doctored so she can't have puppies. Anyway, the point, as I see it, is to be sure to use what we have right now."

"Like what, for instance?"

"Like Joan Luckey and her coyotes. Or John Harris. You could do the same thing."

"You mean, take Laska when I speak at schools and meetings?"

LASKA

"Why not? You've taken porcupines and squirrels and skunks. Why not a wolf? You can probably get her to howl on command. You're always trying to justify having her, anyway. Maybe this is your chance."

Peg's kindergarten class had come to visit Laska a couple of times. So had a number of other school youngsters. They'd always enjoyed meeting her. She'd ham it up in high style too—greeting everybody in sight, sometimes jumping right over the head of a toddler or two, and voicing her feelings in a short, low, companionable howl. Perhaps it was, indeed, worth a try.

So the next time I packed my paraphernalia I also packed Laska. She looked a bit overwhelming in the rear seat of our new little Chevy Nova, but it was worth the effort. The youngsters loved it.

Often when I arrive for a talk, there's a delegation there to meet me. As many as a dozen students have flocked out to the car in a flying wedge of enthusiasm. They want to carry everything: projector, slides, books, extension cords. I give them all but the projector: its delicate innards might not stand such exuberance.

The sight of Laska's piercing eyes in that back seat usually takes a few bubbles off their effervescence. It's only temporary, however: that tail waving wildly, the pink tongue ready to give everybody in the school a lick, the glad-to-see-you look gets rid of any misgivings they might have. From then on, our wolfdog finds a whole school of new friends—one classroom at a time.

❦ ❦ ❦

It has been an education all around. Laska had never had much experience with crowds, but willingly took her place as the center of attention. The youngsters, used to stories about *Little Red Riding Hood* and the *Three Little Pigs,* learned a whole new side to the wolf—although I had to help exercise their imagination because she is the wrong color.

Sometimes it took more than imagination. When I asked one class how they felt about wolves after meeting Laska, one youngster said, "Aw, that ain't no wolf."

Which would have amounted to mutiny in the classroom if Laska hadn't saved the day. She often howls when I look at her and nod my head. So I tried it now—and she obliged. It was just a little howl, but it was her first of the day and perfectly timed.

The boy's eyes widened. "Gee," he said, "I'm sorry!"

I learned a lot myself. Those youngsters volunteered all kinds of refreshing comments. Many of them came forth with tales about pets of their own, "I had a dog once," a third grader confided, "but that was when I was young."

Another time a boy lamented the loss of a dog that had died of a heart attack. This prompted a second boy to inform the class of a puppy that was subject to nervous breakdowns. When I asked him about it further he clarified things. "My puppy pees on the floor when he gets excited," he said.

A second-grade girl had a real wolf story, of sorts.

LASKA

"My sister and I almost heard a wolf in the woods in Maine," she announced. "Boy, did we run!"

One lad thought we should be made aware of his special pet. "We've got a dog that's over a hundred years old," he announced.

"Over a hundred?" I asked. "You mean compared to a human being because dogs get old faster?"

"Nope. A hundred years," he stated flatly.

This silenced the whole class for a moment. Apparently nobody was able to top that one.

But a second boy could bottom it: "Huh! We've got a dog that's younger than a puppy!"

The youngsters usually want to know Laska's age. When I tell them, they compare it to their own pets or to themselves.

I'll not soon forget one girl's comment; she'd come to visit our house when Laska was four years of age.

"Too bad she's too old to have puppies," she sympathized.

"What do you mean?" I asked.

"Well, my father says each year of a dog's life is like seven of ours. So if she's four, she's twenty-eight. And that's *old!*"

Often, a few days after I've visited a classroom or a group has come to see me, I find a sheaf of thank-you letters in the mail. I cherish every letter—smudges, misspellings, and all. Each gets an individual reply.

This used to be a monumental task until I hit upon

the idea of jotting my answer on the note and sending it right back. In this way the youngster gets both ends of the correspondence.

Many of these letters are too interesting merely to send back and forget. So I copy an important paragraph or two on file cards. I'd like to share a few with you.

"Thank you for showing us Laska. I had a puppy once but he fell in the river. Then he drowned. I guess he was allergic to water."

"We have a doxtion. You know, the hotdog dog."

"I like weekends because then I can sleep on the sofa with my dog Flash. The rest of the time I sleep with mother, but Uncle Paul comes on weekends."

"Once we had a puppy but he thought everywhere was the bathroom. We do not have him any more."

Children are forever eager to share stories of their pets with me. Nine-year-old Marsha told me of the wish for a pet of her own:

"We would like to have a dog but my father says no. He says it would eat a hole in his wallet. Why is this?"

Another had less than perfect success, apparently, when she confessed that "I love animals and many have died."

Still another hoped I'd help solve a puzzling problem—probably a matter of communication:

"Our cat had more kittens. My father and mother will not tell me why. I hope you can tell me because you know about things."

LASKA

Nine-year-old Michael was comfortably situated, apparently, with his pets. He merely hoped I'd be able to enjoy them, too, when he wrote the invitation to "come and see my geese." Then he added, as an afterthought: "and my parents."

A lad named Joshua, wishing to share our visit with his infant sister, wrote and asked me to "Please come back agin so my little sister can here you some day. Wen you came before she was not even out yet."

One girl informed me that "I was sorry not to get to your talk in the evening. But what you told us in the morning was enough."

Still another decided "It must be great to have lots of wild life like you."

Laska, understandably, was often the star of the show. As I tried to relate the friendly, black and white creature to that mysterious denizen of the deep woods, I found varying degrees of success. "You and Laska certainly helped us to feel kind toward wolves," announced one girl. "If I ever find one in the woods I will try to make it feel better. But I am not sure I would bring it home."

Her classmate had a realistic view of wolves in the wilderness: "We all loved to see your wolf dog Laska. But it makes me so sad to think that wolves are almost gone and in a few years they will be instinct."

Another interesting play on words was afforded by a boy who announced to the class that if he ever found a wolf that was sick "I would take it to a vegetarian." There was also the time, when two children were visiting us here at our house, that one explained to the other that "the sharp teeth on Laska are sort of like the tallows on the feet of hawks and owls."

I guess the best example of the right word in the wrong place was provided by the "Class Secratery," as she signed herself, after I had made a visit to a private school in Williamstown, Massachusetts. "We have had a meeting," she confided, "and we have all voted that you and Laska are certainly supper."

Regarding the predatory nature of wild creatures, I was informed that "the reason humans kill is to murder someone. But now I know a wolf is more serious than that." Fifth grader Alan decided that "after meeting Laska and learning all those things about wolves I know one thing. If I ever meet a wolf with a gun I would shoot myself first."

One letter contained a dime. It was "to help with all the trouble the wolve is haveing."

So the message gets across, somehow. And, at least, a small portion of it remains over the months. It is gratifying to have some child stop me on the street or in the hall of a school where I've visited previously with a joyous "Hi Mr. Rood! Remember me? How's Laska?"

One evening I was showing some slides after a day with the youngsters. We had scheduled a short walk after school, but gusty winds and bad weather prevented it. They got worse as afternoon turned into evening. And when I was halfway through the slideshow, the power failed. My microphone went dead. The projector quit. The only lights in the school auditorium were the emergency lamps at each corner. I couldn't go on with the show until power was restored.

I hoped it would be only a few minutes. The kids enjoyed the little emergency hugely: they whistled and screamed and had a wonderful time.

At last the lights came on. We finished the show. But a few days later I was reminded of it by a small girl's note of thanks, ". . . and the best part of it all," she wrote, "was when the lights went out and we could not hear you."

Those school engagements with Laska have made countless friends. So have the visits to our home by schoolchildren, natural history groups and Sunday School classes. Sometimes, especially with the very young, it's quite a demand on their credibility to ask them to believe she's part wolf.

The white paws and belly, the black ears, heavily furred inside with white, the white muzzle and startling blue eyes contrast with the blackish head, back and upper surface of tail. And hardly any of it seems to fit the traditional grizzled gray of the timber wolf.

Her shape is right, however, and her size. She outweighs most Siberian husky females, and even many males. But it's her actions, her voice, the quiet pad-pad-pad of those restless feet and the long legs that mark the wolf in her.

So we have found a purpose for her at last. One of the biggest tragedies in nature, I believe, is for any living thing to be completely wasted. And, as long as the wild creature is locked forever in our wolfdog, it is good to be able to put it to use.

She fills a couple of other little niches here, as well. Chickadees and tree swallows prize the dense white tufts of fur that come out as she sheds her coat. I've even seen a chickadee alight right on her gray flank and take the bit of fur of its choice. It probably uses it in its nest.

Interestingly, Laska tolerates the attentions of these birds. Perhaps, in pulling out the tufts of hair, they get rid of an itchy spot. Certainly when she's shedding she spends a good share of her time scratching.

Our hope for another use for her involved that ring-tailed bandit, the raccoon. Each summer these animals sample the sweet corn when it's in the "milk" stage. They pull apart one ear, eat a few kernels and go on to another. In this way a family of 'coons can wreck a whole corn patch overnight.

So we tied Laska at the edge of the garden, near the rows of corn. There; that'd fix those raccoons. Her presence should keep them away so the corn would be safe.

In the morning we looked out to see if our sentinel had done her job. She lay in the grass by the garden, snoozing in the morning sun. There was not a sign of any raccoon.

Then as we peered closer we saw an impressive

sight. The cornstalks, every one of them, looked as if each had suffered its own personal hurricane. During the night she had sniffed out the ripest ears. Pulling them away from the stalks, she had taken them to the garden edge. There she had leisurely chewed them to bits.

Luckily the far ends of the rows had been out of her reach. Since she'd done all the damage she could within range, we tied her in the same spot for the next few nights.

And it worked. Her large presence apparently caused the raccoons to change their minds. So she helped us save the corn anyway—even if it turned out to be only half a crop.

She's a little more valuable in the winter. Sometimes, when guests bring a tot along with them, we'll hitch her up and give a few dog-sled rides. It's the thrill of a lifetime for the youngster. Besides, it helps Laska with her exercise.

Lacking a passenger or the time for the sled, Peg and I take her for at least one walk a day. Or, if we figure she needs a good workout, we drive the car through the meadow while she races to keep up with it.

I've tried to run with her myself. However, my best effort is no match for those tireless legs. Although wolves are not notably swift—seldom exceeding thirty miles an hour in a quick dash, and only twenty for the next few minutes—it is their endurance that makes them such superb runners. The best human being can cover a mile in about four minutes—which, even if kept up, would be merely fifteen miles an hour.

So, while I do my utmost, all I can do is keep up with her. With her it is a game. If I get even half a step ahead she'll merely lope a little faster. And if I drop back she'll slow down accordingly. Hence, slow or fast, I can wear myself out while she just trots along at little more than idling speed.

People often look at those bleak white eyes and that powerful body. They consider the width of jaw, those long teeth, that arresting howl that is so startling the first time one hears it. "Now, *there*," they say, in a tone of respect, "is what should be a great watchdog!"

And so she should be. But, again, there's that word "should." The reality is she'd do a great job in keeping other dogs off her territory.

But—an intruder? She'd howl, yes, and stare with those arresting eyes. She would also approach with all eighty pounds of bone and muscle and sinews. And then—she'd lick the stranger's hand.

Well, there is one time she'd be a good watchdog, at that: if somebody accidentally stepped on her.

Now, as I pen these words, that wolfdog sleeps peacefully in front of the fireplace. No fire is burning, of course. Her feet are twitching, her ears flick back and forth. Perhaps she's chasing an imaginary moose in her dreams. Perhaps she's escaping from an irate mother bison, intent on shielding her calf. Perhaps she's off again after another woodchuck to bring in for breakfast.

Or perhaps our blue-eyed wolf is running through a seated crowd of delighted youngsters, cavorting and leaping and helping a few young minds learn something beyond *Little Red Riding Hood.*

Years ago, when Peg and I had reluctantly decided to have our wolfdog deprived of her capacity to bear puppies, I had silently promised I'd make up the loss to her somehow. And now, as I consider the many friends she has made—the people, young and old, who show a new and dramatically changed attitude toward the wolf—I feel the debt, at least in part, has been paid.

DATE DUE			
6/30/80			